Series / Number 07-047

CANONICAL CORRELATION ANALYSIS

Uses and Interpretation

BRUCE THOMPSON
University of New Orleans

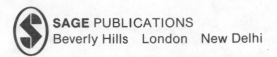

SAGE PUBLICATIONS
Beverly Hills   London   New Delhi

For information address:

SAGE Publications, Inc.
275 South Beverly Drive
Beverly Hills, California 90212

SAGE Publications India Pvt. Ltd.
C-236 Defence Colony
New Delhi 110 024, India

SAGE Publications Ltd
28 Banner Street
London EC1Y 8QE, England

International Standard Book Number 0-8039-2392-9

Library of Congress Catalog Card No. 84-051703

SECOND PRINTING, 1985

When citing a professional paper, please use the proper form. Remember to cite the
correct Sage University Paper series title and include the paper number. One of the
following formats can be adapted (depending on the style manual used):

(1) IVERSEN, GUDMUND R. and NORPOTH, HELMUT (1976) "Analysis of
Variance." Sage University Paper series on Quantitative Applications in the Social
Sciences, 07-001. Beverly Hills and London: Sage Pubns.

OR

(2) Iversen, Gudmund R. and Norpoth, Helmut. 1976. *Analysis of Variance.* Sage
University Paper series on Quantitative Applications in the Social Sciences, series no.
07-001. Beverly Hills and London: Sage Pubns.

CONTENTS

Series Editor's Introduction

Canonical correlation analysis has been available to researchers in theory for roughly 50 years. However, computer programs that perform the analysis have only recently become widely accessible. The automation of the analysis together with recent methodological refinements (e.g., rotation and backward variable elimination) have meant that, in the words of one team of authors, the method has "come of age."

Professor Thompson has written a clear and concise introduction to this old but still emerging technique. The presentation includes the liberal use of examples. In addition to providing a concrete basis for discussion, the tabled data will allow the reader to verify results and to follow along with the discussion by also analyzing the examples. The text is also remarkable for its currency. A broad literature that crosses various disciplines is well represented in the work.

One feature of the book is particularly commendable, given the emphasis of this Sage series on introductory presentations of the various tools available to behavioral scientists: Professor Thompson notes that canonical correlation analysis is a general analytic method of which other parametric significance testing methods (t-tests, ANOVA, regression, etc.) represent special cases. This notion provides an important pedagogic perspective to students, for whom the perspective can provide a framework for then relating these various methods.

As Professor Thompson notes, canonical correlation analysis is a sophisticated technique. Yet the method in many cases is only as complex as the reality social scientists investigate, and the method can honor that reality and can accurately represent some of its dynamics. This readable and lucid introduction will place an important methodology in the hands of a growing number of researchers.

–John L. Sullivan
Series Co-Editor

CANONICAL CORRELATION ANALYSIS
Uses and Interpretation

BRUCE THOMPSON
University of New Orleans

1. INTRODUCTION

Some 15 years ago, in a now classic *Psychological Bulletin* article, Cohen (1968: 426) noted that "if you should say to a mathematical statistician that you have discovered that linear multiple regression analysis and the analysis of variance (and covariance) are identical systems, he would mutter something like, 'Of course—general linear model,' and you might have trouble maintaining his attention. If you should say this to a typical psychologist, you would be met with incredulity, or worse. Yet it is true, and in its truth lie possibilities for more relevant and therefore more powerful exploitation of research data." Since Cohen's article several authors have written textbooks that emphasize the use of regression models in analysis of variance designs (e.g., Edwards, 1979). Perhaps as a result, the general linear model "has been extensively used" in recent research (Willson, 1982: 1).

However, Baggaley (1981: 129) has noted that canonical correlation analysis, and not regression analysis, is the most general case of the general linear model. Knapp (1978: 410) demonstrated this in detail and concluded that "virtually all of the commonly encountered parametric tests of significance can be treated as special cases of canonical correlation analysis, which is the general procedure for investigating the relationships between two sets of variables." In a similar vein Fornell (1978: 168) notes, "Multiple regression, MANOVA and ANOVA, and multiple discriminant analysis can all be shown to be special cases of canonical analysis. Principal components analysis is also in the inner family circle." Although the recognition that ANOVA designs are special cases of regression brought increased use of regression models, the recognition that canonical correlation analysis is the most general case of the general linear model has not yet produced a corresponding increase in the use of canonical techniques.

Trends in Use of Canonical Analysis

In a 1973 publication, Kerlinger and Pedhazur noted:

> One does not readily find research studies that have used canonical
> correlation. In earlier years the prohibitive calculations involved
> and general unfamiliarity with the method of course inhibited its
> use. Today, computer facilities and canonical correlation pro-
> grams are available. One suspects, therefore, that researchers are
> still unfamiliar with it [p. 345].

That same year Tatsuoka (p. 299) concurred and suggested, "Genuine
substantive applications of canonical correlation analysis are hard to
come by. . . . In all fairness, any substantive application of this rather
complicated technique represents a gallant effort worthy of note." More
recently, Thorndike (1977: 76) indicated that,

> given the substantial theoretical literature on canonical analysis, it
> is surprising to find that the technique has seen relatively infre-
> quent use by researchers studying substantive problems. Instances
> where the methods of canonical analysis have been applied rather
> than studied for their own sake are relatively rare (but on the
> increase).

And as recently as 1981 Baggaley (p. 129) reported, "It is rather
surprising that canonical correlation has not been used very often to
analyze behavioral data."

Empirical reviews of the literature suggest that these perceptions
accurately reflect methodological practice. For example, Willson,
(1980) reviewed 10 volumes of the *American Educational Research
Journal* and found only seven applications of the technique in 280
articles reporting 480 technique applications. Apropos of Kerlinger and
Pedhazur (1973), Willson (1980: 8) reported also that "a perusal of 18
education research method texts currently available (virtually a
complete set of currently marketed texts)" located only one or two texts
that discussed canonical correlation analysis.

In addition to limited awareness of canonical methods, at least two
other reasons for the limited use of canonical methods have been cited
(Balon and Philport, 1977: 200; Thorndike, 1977: 76). First, Baggaley

(1981: 123) suggests that "the mathematical symbolism involved in the textbooks presently available on this subject discourages all but the most persistent practitioners from attempting to learn this material." Second, Thompson (1980a: 1, 16-17) notes that another

> reason why the technique is rarely used involves the difficulties which can be encountered in trying to interpret canonical results. . . . The neophyte student of canonical correlation analysis may be overwhelmed by the myriad coefficients which the procedure produces. . . . [But] canonical correlation analysis produces results which can be theoretically rich, and if properly implemented the procedure can adequately capture some of the complex dynamics involved in educational reality.

Nevertheless, the technique and recent extensions of the technique do have their advocates. Kerlinger (1973: 652) suggests that "some research problems almost demand canonical analysis." Cooley and Lohnes (1971: 176) suggest that "it is the simplest model that can begin to do justice to this difficult problem of scientific generalization." Krus, Reynolds, and Krus (1976: 725) argue that, "Dormant for nearly half a century, Hotelling's (1935, 1936) canonical variate analysis has come of age. The principal reason behind its resurrection was its computerization and inclusion in major statistical packages." Thus Wood and Erskine (1976) were able to review more than 30 applications of these methods.

Questions Addressed by Canonical Analysis

The purpose of this paper is to present canonical correlation analysis with a view toward making the methods more widely available to social scientists. Particular attention will be devoted to relatively recent developments. Notwithstanding Levine's (1977: 8) assertion that "especially with respect to canonical correlation, there seem to be relatively few remaining puzzles to be solved," several important puzzles regarding this methodology have been both recognized and then resolved during the last several years.

Given that canonical correlation analysis can be as complex as a reality in which most causes have multiple effects and most effects are multiply caused, an "advance organizer" regarding some of the research questions that can be addressed using canonical analysis may be helpful. Among other purposes, canonical correlation analysis can be employed to investigate the following research questions:

(1) To what extent can one set of two or more variables be predicted or "explained" by another set of two or more variables?

(2) What contribution does a single variable make to the explanatory power of the set of variables to which the variable belongs?

(3) To what extent does a single variable contribute to predicting or "explaining" the composite of the variables in the variable set to which the variable does *not* belong?

(4) What different dynamics are involved in the ability of one variable set to "explain" in different ways different portions of the other variable set?

(5) What relative power do different canonical functions have to predict or explain relationships?

(6) How stable are canonical results across samples or sample subgroups?

(7) How closely do obtained canonical results conform to expected canonical results?

After various canonical coefficients and methods are discussed, the limits of canonical analysis will be considered and the canonical results that address these questions will be summarized (see Table 29).

2. THE LOGIC OF CANONICAL ANALYSIS

Hotelling (1935) originally developed the logic for conventional canonical correlation analysis. More mathematical (Cooley and Lohnes, 1971: 168-200) and more intuitive (Bentler and Huba, 1982: 22-25) explanations of the technique are readily available. Most computer software packages now include a routine for performing canonical analysis.

Canonical correlation analysis is employed to study relationships between two variable sets when each variable set consists of at least two variables. Thus Table 1 presents the data for what is the simplest canonical case, since only two criterion variables, X and Y, and only two predictor variables, A and B, are involved. Of course, these data are

TABLE 1
Hypothetical Data Set

Case	X	Y	A	B
1	1 (−0.72)	9 (+1.36)	4 (+0.08)	6 (+0.33)
2	5 (+1.90)	4 (−0.15)	0 (−1.02)	8 (+0.88)
3	3 (+0.59)	9 (+1.36)	6 (+0.64)	0 (−1.33)
4	3 (+0.59)	4 (−0.15)	6 (+0.64)	9 (+1.16)
5	3 (+0.59)	3 (−0.45)	9 (+1.46)	0 (−1.33)
6	2 (−0.07)	2 (−0.76)	9 (+1.46)	0 (−1.33)
7	2 (−0.07)	0 (−1.36)	2 (−0.47)	9 (+1.16)
8	0 (−1.38)	2 (−0.76)	0 (−1.02)	5 (+0.06)
9	0 (−1.38)	9 (+1.36)	1 (−0.74)	6 (+0.33)
10	2 (−0.07)	3 (−0.45)	0 (−1.02)	5 (+0.06)

NOTE: Z-score equivalents of the unstandardized data are presented in parentheses.

presented only for the purposes of discussion, since the hypothetical sample size (n = 10) is absurdly small. (Less mathematically oriented readers may wish to skip the following section, or may want to return to the section after first developing a better intuitive understanding of canonical methods.)

Canonical Calculations

The first step in a canonical correlation analysis involves the calculation of the intervariable correlation matrix presented in Table 2. A symmetric matrix of reduced rank equal to the number of variables in the smaller of the two variable sets is then derived from the intervariable correlation matrix (see Cooley and Lohnes, 1971: 176, for details) in the manner portrayed in Table 3. The eigenvalues of matrix A computed in Table 3 each represent a squared canonical correlation coefficient. Since the number of eigenvalues that can be calculated for such a matrix equals the number of rows (or columns) in the matrix, it should be clear that the maximum number of canonical correlation coefficients that can be derived for a data set equals the number of variables in the smaller of the two variable sets. Because in this example both variable sets consist of two variables, only two canonical correlation coefficients can be calculated.

The matrix manipulations presented in Table 3 are not important in themselves. The manipulations are important, however, to the extent that they will facilitate intuitive recognition of linkages between

TABLE 2
Correlation Matrix

	X		Y	A		B
X	1.000		−.165	.227		.004
		R11			R12	
Y	−.165		1.00	.014		−.139
A	.227		.014	1.000		−.641
		R21			R22	
B	.004		−.139	−.641		1.000

principal components analysis and canonical correlation analysis (Bartlett, 1948). A full-rank principal components analysis of the Table 2 correlation matrix, R, will yield four uncorrelated function equations that have come to be called *factors*. The sum of the four eigenvalues associated with the analysis will equal the rank of the matrix, that is, 4; this sum divided by the number of rows or columns in the matrix, that is, the rank of the matrix, will equal 1, which correctly suggests that a full-rank principal components analysis of a correlation matrix will contain 100 percent of the variance in the correlation matrix. Each eigenvalue can be consulted to determine which of the factors contain enough of the variance from the analyzed matrix to warrant interpretation.

A full-rank principal components analysis of matrix A derived from R through the manipulations presented in Table 3 will yield two uncorrelated function equations. The sum of the two eigenvalues associated with matrix A can be no larger than the rank of the matrix, that is, here 2; the sum of these eigenvalues divided by the rank of the analyzed matrix indicates how much of the possible variance in A the computed functions contain. In fact, these eigenvalues are squared canonical correlation coefficients and will sum to the rank of the matrix only when all possible canonical functions involve perfect relationships. Of course, these rather special eigenvalues can also be consulted to determine which functions may warrant interpretation.

Thus principal components analysis and canonical correlation analysis are similar in that similar mathematics are employed in the techniques. However, different matrices (respectively, R or A) are actually subjected to the mathematics. Even this difference could be

TABLE 3
Matrix Manipulations

			R_{22}^{-1}		R_{21}	R_{11}		R_{12}^{-1}	= A	
1.000	−.641	−1	.227	.014	1.000	−.165	−1	.227	.004	
−.641	1.000		.004	−.139	−.165	1.000		.014	−.139	
1.699	1.090		.227	.014	1.028	.170		.227	.004	
1.090	1.699		.004	−.139	.170	1.028		.014	−.139	
			.391	−.128	1.028	.170		.227	.004	
			.255	−.222	.170	1.028		.014	−.139	
					.380	−.065		.227	.004	
					.224	−.184		.014	−.139	
								.086	.011	
								.048	.027	

overemphasized since A is itself derived from R. But A is computed from R in a rather special way.

The computation of A honors membership in variable sets so that the relationships between the two sets of variables can be better understood. As Reynolds and Jackosfsky (1981, p. 662) explain:

Given the research purpose of canonical analysis, namely, the study of the interrelationship of two variable sets, the Rxy [$R21$] quadrant is of primary interest. This becomes clear when the canonical problem is redefined, by taking into account interrelationships in both Rxx [$R22$] and Ryy [$R11$] in order to fully evaluate the correlations in Rxy.

Thus Cooley and Lohnes (1971: 169) note that "the factor model selects linear functions of tests that have maximum variances, subject to the restriction of orthogonality. The canonical model selects linear functions that have maximum covariances between domains, subject again to restrictions or orthogonality." Similarly, Tatsuoka (1971: 183) argues that "the technique may therefore be loosely characterized as a sort of 'double-barrelled principal components analysis.' It identifies the 'components' of one set of variables that are most highly related (linearly) to the 'components' of the other set of variables."

TABLE 4
Calculation of Composites

Case	ZX	F1	ZY	F2	Criterion Composite	Predictor Composite		ZA	F3	ZB	F4
1	(-0.72)	(F1) +	(+1.36)	(F2) =	-0.97	+0.42	=	(+0.08)	(F3) +	(+0.33)	(F4)
2	(+1.90)	(F1) +	(-0.15)	(F2) =	+1.82	-0.49	=	(-1.02)	(F3) +	(+0.88)	(F4)
3	(+0.59)	(F1) +	(+1.36)	(F2) =	+0.26	-0.43	=	(+0.64)	(F3) +	(-1.33)	(F4)
4	(+0.59)	(F1) +	(-0.15)	(F2) =	+0.59	+1.92	=	(+0.64)	(F3) +	(+1.16)	(F4)
5	(+0.59)	(F1) +	(-0.45)	(F2) =	+0.65	+0.64	=	(+1.46)	(F3) +	(-1.33)	(F4)
6	(-0.07)	(F1) +	(-0.76)	(F2) =	+0.10	+0.64	=	(+1.46)	(F3) +	(-1.33)	(F4)
7	(-0.07)	(F1) +	(-1.36)	(F2) =	+0.23	+0.49	=	(-0.47)	(F3) +	(+1.16)	(F4)
8	(-1.38)	(F1) +	(-0.76)	(F2) =	-1.14	-1.27	=	(-1.02)	(F3) +	(+0.06)	(F4)
9	(-1.38)	(F1) +	(+1.36)	(F2) =	-1.59	-0.65	=	(-0.74)	(F3) +	(+0.33)	(F4)
10	(-0.07)	(F1) +	(-0.45)	(F2) =	+0.04	-1.27	=	(-1.02)	(F3) +	(+0.06)	(F4)

NOTE: The canonical function coefficients are as follows: F1 = +0.94; F2 = −0.22; F3 = +1.30; F4 = +0.94.

Canonical Correlation as a Bivariate Coefficient

Conventional canonical correlation analysis investigates the degree of relationship between two sets of variables. In effect, the analysis proceeds by initially collapsing each person's scores on the variables in each variable set into a single composite variable. The simple or bivariate correlation between the two composite scores (one for each of the two variable sets) is a canonical correlation.

However, the composite scores are computed subject to a very special restriction. The composite scores are derived to maximize the relationship between the two variable sets they represent. This "optimization" is performed by "weighting" each person's data and then summating the weighted scores in each variable set. The weights can be either negative or positive numbers and are simply multiplied times the scores for each person. These weights are called *function coefficients* and are the same as beta weights in a regression analysis or pattern coefficients in a factor analysis. The composites derived using these "best possible" weights are called *variate scores*. A squared canonical correlation coefficient indicates the proportion of variance that the two composites derived from the two variable sets linearly share.

Table 4 provides an illustration of these calculations. Note, for example, that the criterion variate for the first canonical function equals .94 and −.22, and that the criterion variate scores for this function are

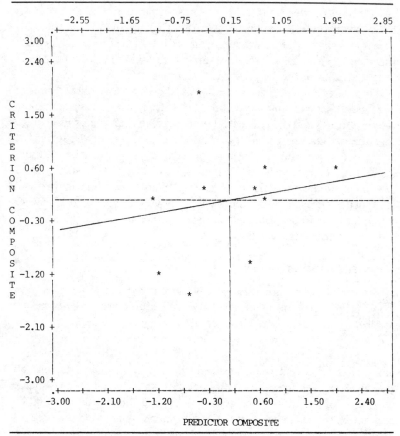

Figure 1: Scattergram of the Two Composites

reported in the column headed "Criterion Composite." The table only presents the coefficients for the first canonical function, although it has already been noted that a second function could have been calculated. The canonical correlation is the bivariate correlation between the two table columns headed "Criterion Composite" and "Predictor Composite." These 10 pairs of values are plotted in the Figure 1 scattergram. The figure also presents the regression line for the two sets of 10 composites. Since the composites are themselves also in Z score form, the regression line passes through the mean of both composites, that is, the X-Y intercept, and the line's slope (.305) equals the bivariate correlation between the two composites and also the canonical correlation between the two variable sets. Thus the figure illustrates in a concrete fashion Huba, Newcomb, and Bentler's (1981: 292) statement that "the canonical correlation model assesses the way in which weighted sums of the original variables interrelate."

The reader is encouraged to verify that the Table 4 weights are indeed "optimal." Vary any one of the function coefficients slightly, recompute the composites and then the correlation between the composites. Notice that the further one deviates from the optimal weights the lower the correlation between the composite scores becomes. The optimal character of the function coefficients suggests the basic logic of canonical analysis—if there is no appreciable relationship between composites derived using the best possible weights, then no other weights can yield a higher correlation, and the variable sets are simply not related to an appreciable degree.

Required Statistical Assumptions

Statistical procedures are usually formulated based upon certain assumptions that must be met if the procedures are to be correctly applied. It is important, however, to distinguish those assumptions required when the analysis is conducted for descriptive purposes as against situations in which inferential tests of statistical significance are conducted. Since matrix A is derived from the intervariable correlation matrix R in all applications, all applications require that reasonable estimates of the "true" correlations among the variables can be computed. Thus at least three assumptions must be met even in descriptive applications.

First, it must be assumed that the measurement error of the variables is minimal since low reliability tends to attenuate the entries in R. By definition, chance or error variation will attenuate product-moment coefficients, since these indices only reflect systematic covariation (Allen and Yen, 1979: 75). Of course, poor sampling of subjects, if it leads to truncated or restricted variance, will also attenuate the entries in R, and so a second required assumption is that the variances of the variables are not restricted. However, the consequences of both forms of attenuation can be minimized with correction formulae (e.g., Guilford, 1965: 480) if the researcher is alert to possible problems. Furthermore, as argued for the related factor analytic case (Thompson, 1982c: 2-4), it is also comforting to note that canonical functions tend to be constructed from the "true score" components of variables.

The third assumption involves the variables as they are considered in pairs; the magnitudes of the coefficients in the correlation matrix must not be attenuated by large differences in the shapes of the distributions for the variables. It is important to emphasize that this assumption does not require that the variables be normally distributed as long as there is no substantial attenuation associated with distribution differences, regardless of what these distributions may be. This point is noteworthy because a requirement of distribution normality would preclude use of would preclude use of noncontinuous data in a canonical analysis.

Cooley and Lohnes (1976: 209) provide an example application of the technique in a study involving several nominally scaled variables. Similarly, Maxwell (1961: 271) notes:

> In this article attention is drawn to the fact that the theory of canonical variate analysis, widely used with continuous variables, can also be employed when the variables are dichotomous. The theory is then briefly reviewed and is demonstrated by an example in which canonical variates for discriminating between three groups of psychiatric patients are set up using four dichotomous variables.

But canonical analysis involving variables with different levels of scale may inherently violate to some degree the third assumption for the use of the technique. Of course, the more common use of canonical methods with intervally scaled variables also may or may not involve more serious violations of this assumption.

When the researcher has in hand data from a reasonably representative sample from a population, as may be the case with a random sample, inferences about population parameters can be investigated by applying conventional tests of statistical significance. In this application, and only in this nondescriptive application, a fourth assumption must be met. As Marascuilo and Levin (1983: 203) note,

> The multivariate normal distribution is somewhat hidden throughout multivariate methods. It is not required in the estimation and data description aspects of the theory. Its impact and role, however, are basic to the inference procedures of multivariate analysis and it is here that it must be assumed. There are no satisfactory tests of its truth in any one situation.

The absence of a practical, readily usable test statistic that can be employed to test this fourth assumption suggests a paradox. If the researcher knows that the population distributions are multivariate normal, the researcher probably also knows the other population parameters, and would not need to apply any test statistics involving the canonical results in the first place. Alternatively, if the researcher is not certain that the population distributions are multivariate normal, little can be done to resolve this uncertainty short of gathering data from the entire population of interest.

Therefore researchers will generally be uncertain as to whether or not they have met the distribution assumption of canonical correlation analysis. It is important to emphasize, however, that examining the univariate or the bivariate distributions will not conclusively resolve this uncertainty. Multivariate distributions can be nonnormal even when all subsets of univariate or bivariate distributions are normal, just as a bivariate distribution may be nonnormal even when both the individual variables are individually distributed in a normal manner.

One reason for limited discussion of the multivariate normal distribution is itself noteworthy. There is a basic theorem in mathematical statistics called the *multivariate central limit theorem*. This theorem suggests that when sample size is "large," certain indices derived from the variables will be normally distributed even when the variables are not themselves distributed in a multivariate normal manner. This assurance can be relied upon to justify the application of test statistics in a canonical correlation analysis whenever the sample is large. However, there is no generally accepted rule for determining when a sample is large enough to justify invoking the theorem. Consequently, it is generally desirable to obtain the largest possible sample size, since this tends to justify invoking the theorem. However, it is important to note that the stability of canonical functions and interpretations of them also presume large samples even in descriptive applications, since least squares (i.e., correlational) methods do tend to capitalize on sampling error.

In short, as McLaughlin and Otto (1981: 8) note, "In general, it can be said that canonical correlation requires the same set of assumptions employed in the more commonly utilized general linear model techniques, such as multiple correlation, regression, and factor analysis, but also shares the robustness of these techniques with regard to violations of those assumptions."

Computing Significance Tests

Several test statistics are available when the researcher wishes to test the statistical significance of a null hypothesis of no relationship between the criterion and the predictor variable sets. For example, Rao (1951) developed a test that yields an approximation associated with the *F* distribution. However, the most commonly used procedure is attributed to Bartlett (1941) and yields an approximation associated with the chi-square distribution. As Darlington, Weinberg, and Walberg (1973: 441) note:

> Schatzoff (1966) has published tables of coefficients for correcting the values of chi-square computed by this formula, but the coefficients are so close to unity for values of N above 50 that Bartlett's test can be regarded as highly accurate for these sample sizes. Furthermore, the Bartlett test is always on the conservative side.

Nevertheless, the corrections are also tabled in Timm (1975).

Since the calculations involved in Bartlett's test of the omnibus hypothesis are rather complicated, and since the calculations are automated in commonly available statistics packages and do not facilitate insight into canonical methods themselves, the required calculations will be treated here in a rather cursory fashion. The chi-square test statistic can be calculated as follows:

$$\chi^2 = -(n - .5(v_1 + v_2 + 1)) \log_e(\text{lambda}),$$

where n = the number of subjects,

v_1 = the number of variables in set 1,

v_2 = the number of variables in set 2,

lambda = $(1 - R^2c1)(1 - R^2c2)...(1 - R^2cp)$ for each
of *p* possible R^2c's.

Of course, as suggested previously, *p* will be equal to the number of variables in the smaller of the two variable sets. The required calculations associated with the omnibus hypothesis for the Table 1 data are presented in Table 5. The degrees of freedom for the omnibus hypothesis equals the number of variables in each set times each other (here, 2 × 2 = 4). The degrees of freedom calculations for subsequent hypotheses are illustrated in Table 6 for a data set which will be discussed momentarily.

Marascuilo and Levin (1983: 187) note that it is quite possible to reject the omnibus null hypothesis that all eigenvalues (i.e., squared

TABLE 5
Omnibus Chi-Square Computations

$$-(10 - .5 (2 + 2 + 1)) \ \log_e \ (1 - .093) (1 - .019)$$
$$-(10 - .5 (5)) \ \log_e \ (.890)$$
$$-(10 - 2.5) (-.117)$$
$$(-7.5) (-.117)$$
$$.887$$

TABLE 6
Degrees of Freedom Calculations

Rc	Chi-Square Calculated	df	df Calculation	Critical Chi-Square	Decision
.46	147.38	40	(4+1−1) (10+1−1)	55.76	Reject
.42	93.61	27	(4+1−2) (10+1−2)	40.11	Reject
.34	49.68	16	(4+1−3) (10+1−3)	26.30	Reject
.31	22.35	7	(4+1−4) (10+1−4)	14.07	Reject

NOTE: df for ith Rc = (number of criterion variables + 1 − i) x (number of predictor variables + 1 − i).

canonical correlation coefficients) equal zero and yet find that no single canonical correlation would be judged statistically significant when considered individually. They also propose (pp. 187-188) an intriguing procedure for determining which canonical functions should be retained for interpretation. However, these concerns must be placed in perspective.

Carver (1978) notes that many behavioral scientists incorrectly believe that statistical significance tests inform as to the probability that a result was caused by chance, or as to the probability that a result is reliable, valid, or important. Furthermore, Carver notes that statistical significance is primarily an artifact of sample size. Thus problems are especially likely when these tests are applied to evaluate canonical results.

Large samples are required to invoke the central limit theorem in a canonical analysis. Large samples are required to minimize the tendency of canonical correlation analysis to capitalize on sampling error. So it is quite possible that a statistically significant canonical correlation will be trivial from a substantive point of view. Thus researchers are increasingly employing significance tests only as a *minimal* criterion to use in deciding which canonical functions to interpret.

3. RESULT INTERPRETATION:
ADDITIONAL COEFFICIENTS

When a statistically significant canonical correlation is identified, the researcher will want to interpret the canonical function to determine the extent to which the various variables contributed to the identified multivariate relationship. Several additional coefficients can be calculated to aid in interpretation. The existence of these various additional coefficients is problematic, however, to the extent that a consensus has not yet emerged regarding which terms should be employed to refer to various concepts. As Wood and Erskine (1976: 864) explain:

One researcher's canonical loading becomes another's canonical weight; canonical dimension to one is a canonical variate to another; and, canonical correlation is the relationship between data sets for one, but only the relationship between variates for another.

Structure Coefficients

Canonical *structure coefficients* are particularly important. Thus Meredith (1964: 55) suggested, "If the variables within each set are moderately intercorrelated the possibility of interpreting the canonical variates by inspection of the appropriate regression weights [function coefficients] is practically nil." Kerlinger and Pedhazur (1973: 344) argued, "A canonical correlation analysis also yields weights, which, theoretically at least, are interpreted as regression [beta] weights. These weights [function coefficients] appear to be the weak link in the canonical correlation analysis chain." Similarly, Levine (1977: 20) suggests,

I specifically say that one *has* to do this [interpret structure coefficients] since I firmly believe as long as one wants information about the nature of the canonical correlation relationship, not merely the computation of the [canonical function] scores, one must have the structure matrix [emphasis in original].

A squared canonical structure coefficient represents the proportion of variance linearly shared by a variable with the variable's canonical composite. This fact is not intuitively obvious, since canonical mathematics have historically been presented in matrix algebra form. This makes the technique so abstract that it puts canonical methods beyond

TABLE 7
Selected Cross-Products

Case	ZX	Comp.	Pred. Comp.	Cr. x^a Pred.	$ZX x^b$ Crit.	$ZX x^c$ Pred.
1	−0.72	−0.97	+0.42	−0.41	+0.70	−0.30
2	+1.90	+1.82	−0.49	−0.89	+3.46	−0.93
3	+0.59	+0.26	−0.43	−0.11	+0.15	−0.25
4	+0.59	+0.59	+1.92	+1.13	+0.35	+1.13
5	+0.59	+0.65	+0.64	+0.42	+0.38	+0.38
6	−0.07	+0.10	+0.64	+0.64	−0.01	−0.04
7	−0.07	+0.23	+0.49	+0.11	−0.02	−0.03
8	−1.38	−1.14	−1.27	+1.45	+1.57	+1.75
9	−1.38	−1.59	−0.65	+1.03	+2.19	+0.90
10	−0.07	+0.04	−1.27	−0.05	−0.00	+0.09
Sum				+2.74	+8.78	+2.70

a. 2.74/n - 1 = .305, or the canonical correlation coefficient.
b. 8.78/n - 1 = .976, or the structure coefficient for the variable X on the first of the two possible canonical functions.
c. 2.70/n - 1 = .300, or the index coefficient for the variable X on the first of the two possible canonical functions.

the grasp of some researchers. For example, for this data set the matrix algebra formula for the criterion variable structure coefficients is

$$R_{2\times2} \ W_{2\times2} = S_{2\times2} \qquad [1]$$

where R is the symmetric intraset correlation matrix involving the two criterion variables, W is the matrix of the two criterion variables' function coefficients, and S is the matrix of the two criterion variables' structure coefficients.

However, structure coefficients (and other canonical coefficients) can be both computed and conceptualized in simpler bivariate terms. As some readers may wish to verify, the structure coefficient ($r = .977$) for criterion variable X on the first canonical function also equals the correlation between the Table 7 column headed "ZX" and the column headed "Criterion Composite." The structure coefficient for Y equals the correlation between the Table 7 column headed "ZY" and the column headed "Criterion Composite."

Some matrix algebra must be used to clarify exactly when canonical function and structure coefficients will be the same and when they will necessarily be different. Any symmetric matrix that consists of ones on the diagonal and zeroes in all off-diagonal positions is termed an "identity" matrix. This terminology has evolved because, as Green (1978: 56) notes, "pre- or postmultiplication of a matrix A by I, the identity matrix, leaves the original matrix unchanged." Some reflection on equation 1 suggests that the structure and the function coefficients for a variable set will be equal whenever the variables in the set are perfectly uncorrelated with each other, that is, when the intradomain correlation matrix ($R11$ or $R22$) constitutes an identity matrix. Otherwise the structure and the function coefficients for the variable set will necessarily be different.

The appeal for consultation of structure coefficients can also be based on intuitive linkages with other general linear model techniques. For example, canonical function coefficients are direct analogs of the factor pattern coefficients produced in a principal components analysis; canonical structure coefficients are directly analogous to factor structure coefficients. As Gorsuch (1974: 182) notes, when factors are extracted and then rotated to be orthogonal or uncorrelated, that is, when the correlations among the factors are all zeroes, the factor pattern and the factor structure coefficient matrices are identical. Otherwise the matrices are different and then "the basic matrix for interpreting the factors is the factor structure."

A similar appeal can be made by relating regression and certain canonical coefficients (Thompson and Borrello, in press). Canonical function coefficients are directly analogous to regression beta weights. Although the appeal is probably somewhat less intuitively appealing since fewer researchers are cognizant of regression structure coefficients, regression beta and structure coefficents also are often not equal, though both may be helpful in interpretation (Cooley and Lohnes, 1971: 70).

In the artificial case where one was forced to choose only canonical structure or only canonical function coefficients as the basis for interpretation, a case could certainly be made in favor of the structure coefficients:

> In the first place these weights [function coefficients] may be unstable due to multicollinearity. Some variables may obtain a small weight or even a negative weight because of the fact that the variance in a variable has already been explained by other variables. In this type of situation the weights do not give a clear picture of the relevance of the variables [Kuylen and Verhallen, 1981: 219].

Darlington, Weinberg, and Walberg (1973: 443) approach the problem from a slightly different perspective:

> However, in most cases the choice between the two is dictated by a practical rather than a theoretical consideration: sampling error. By analogy to the situation in multiple regression (Darlington, 1968: 175-177), it can be inferred that the standard errors of weights are often much higher than those of correlations. This is especially true precisely in those cases when the differences between weights and correlations are greatest—when variables within a set are highly intercorrelated.

However, Monte Carlo studies have not yet conclusively demonstrated that structure coefficients are necessarily more stable than function coefficients (Barcikowski and Stevens, 1975; Thorndike, 1976b; Thorndike and Weiss, 1973).

Of course, the forced choice situation is artificial, and actual interpretation decisions must be made in light of purpose, as Thorndike (1976b: 251-252) explains,

> If, by interpretation, one means the independent contributions of the variables to the variance of the composities, (i.e., the variance of this composite is composed of x contribution from variable 1, y contribution from variable 2, etc.), then the weights should be used. However, if one wishes to interpret a composite in terms of its relationships with the observed variables, as is customary in factor analysis, then the loadings [function coefficients] should be used.

Furthermore, in some cases the unstandardized canonical function coefficients (analogous to regression b weights) may even be of interest (Stavig and Acock, 1981). Nevertheless, because the variables in a given variable set are rarely perfectly uncorrelated with each other, and because structure coefficients are particularly helpful in interpreting canonical results in terms of each variable's contribution to the canonical solution, these correlation coefficients must usually be computed as a supplementary aid to the interpretation of canonical function coefficients.

Communality and Adequacy Coefficients

Canonical structure coefficients also form the basis for two other canonical coefficients. Since canonical functions, like principal components or factors, are uncorrelated with each other, the sum of all of a variable's squared structure coefficients equals a canonical *communality coefficient* (Thompson, 1980a: 19; Thorndike, 1977: 83). These values indicate what proportion of each variable's variance is reproducible from the canonical results, that is, how useful each variable was in defining the canonical solution. The average of all the squared structure coefficients for the variables in one set with respect to one function represents a canonical *variate adequacy coefficient*. Essentially these coefficients indicate how "adequately," on the average, a given set of canonical variate scores perform with respect to representing all the variance in the original, unweighted variables in the set.

Redundancy Coefficients and Analysis

In 1968 Stewart and Love suggested that multiplying the variate adequacy coefficient times a squared canonical correlation coefficient yields a *redundancy coefficient* [*Rd*]. The coefficient is an index of the average proportion of variance in the variables in one set that is reproducible from the variables in the other set. As Stewart and Love (1968: 160) suggested, "It is important to note that a relatively strong canonical correlation may obtain between two linear functions, even though these linear functions may not extract significant portions of variance from their respective batteries." Later Wollenberg (1977: 217) pointed out that

the danger of obtaining highly correlated, but unimportant factors in a canonical correlation analysis is especially present when there are two variables, one in each set, which are not characteristic for the whole set, but yet highly correlated with each other. Then one can find a factor pair of essentially unique factors as the first canonical factors.

Table 8 presents just such a correlation matrix. Table 9 presents the variate and structure coefficients from a canonical analysis based on the Table 8 correlation matrix, as well as the multiple correlation coefficients generated from the analysis of the same correlation matrix. Finally, Table 10 presents the redundancy coefficients produced from the canonical results. These results provide a concrete basis for discussion of the psychometric meaning of redundancy coefficients.

Note initially that, on a given function, the two redundancy coefficients for the two variable sets will only equal each other when the adequacy coefficients for the two sets are equal, since the squared

TABLE 8
Hypothetical Correlation Matrix for Hypothethical Case

	X	Y	Z	A	B	C
X	1.0					
Y	.3	1.0				
Z	.0	.0	1.0			
A	.0	.0	.9	1.0		
B	.5	.5	.0	.0	1.0	
C	.3	.5	.0	.0	.4	1.0

canonical correlation is a constant for a given function. Naturally, this rarely occurs in practice, and means that Rd is an "asymmetric" index in that Rd for one variable set rarely will equal Rd for the other variable set. This property may be problematic since the basis for the asymmetric nature of the index is not easily understood and may seem counter-intuitive.

However, the tabled results also suggest that the pooled redundancy coefficient for a given set of variables equals the average multiple correlation for the variables in the set when they are predicted by the variables in the other (see Dawson-Saunders and Doolen, 1981, for a study in which this is demonstrated). This is quite disturbing! The main argument in favor of multivariate techniques is that they *simultaneously* consider all the variables during analysis; this produces results that honor the way in which all the variables presumably interrelate in reality and yields a noninflated experimentwise Type I error rate. Were any of the bivariate correlations involving variables Y and Z considered in computing that the multiple correlation between variable X and the predictor variable set A, B, C equals .2619? As Cramer and Nicewander (1979: 43) point out:

> The redundancy index [for the criterion variables] is not multivar-iate in the strict sense because it is unaffected by the intercorrela-tions of the variables being predicted. The redundancy index is multivariate only in the sense that it involves several criterion variables.

Similarly, Muller (1981: 142) has demonstrated that "redundancy anal-ysis should be treated as evaluating adequacy of regression (prediction) and not association." Cramer and Nicewander (1979) develop several

TABLE 9
Canonical and Regression Results

	Variate			Structure			
	I	II	III	I	II	III	R^2
X	.00	.57	−.88	.00	.77	−.63	.2619
Y	.00	.66	.81	.00	.84	.55	.2976
Z	1.00	.00	.00	1.00	.00	.00	.8100
A	1.00	.00	.00	1.00	.00	.00	.8100
B	.00	.66	−.87	.00	.87	−.49	.3187
C	.00	.53	.95	.00	.80	.60	.2747

NOTE: The squared multiple correlation between X and variables A, B, and C as a set was .2619, and so on. The pooled redundancy coefficient for the criterion variables here equals .2619 + .2976 + .8100 = 1.3695/3 = .4565. The pooled redundancy coefficient for the predictor variables here equals .8100 + .3187 + .2747 = 1.4034/3 = .4678.

truly multivariate indices of association and point out that all of them are functions of the canonical correlation coefficient. Huba, Wingard, and Bentler (1980) report an actual application of several of these indices.

If canonical functions are computed to optimize canonical correlations, then one might question why a researcher would want to consult a coefficient that is not multivariate and is not optimized as part of the analysis. Cooley and Lohnes (1976: 212) cite Miller's (1975) development of a partial sampling distribution for Rd and suggest that Rd is less positively biased than Rc under certain conditions:

> Those researchers who are wary of canonical R because of its strong positive bias when numbers of degrees of freedom are modest may be reassured by Miller's empirical results that the redundancy statistic is much less biased. The corrective which obtains is the tendency of inflated canonical R's to be associated with factors which extract trivial amounts of variance from their batteries.

However, Dawson-Saunders (1982: 141-142) in a large-scale Monte Carlo study found that both Rc and Rd are biased and reported which factors seem to contribute most to these biases:

> The least biased estimates of both the squared canonical correlation coefficients and the canonical redundancy statistics are those that use large sample sizes with moderate to high levels of interbat-

TABLE 10
Summary Statistics

Statistic	I	II	III	Pooled
R_c^2	.81	.40	.05	
Adequacy				
criterion	.33	.43	.23	
predictor	.33	.46	.20	
Rd				
criterion	.27	.17	.01	.4565
predictor	.27	.19	.01	.4678

NOTE: Redundancy coefficients equal adequacy coefficients x squared cononical correlation coefficients (.81 x .33 = .27, etc.).

tery correlations. . . . The investigator may be less concerned with the number of variables in a study, except as this number relates to sample size, and with the degree of relationship among the variables in each individual battery.

However, Dawson-Saunders (1982: 139) did conclude that "the alternative definition of the redundancy as an average squared multiple correlation coefficient led to the suppositon that correction formulae for bias in the squared multiple correlation coefficient might be applicable to the redundancy statistic." Monte Carlo investigations of the corrections found that the corrections were indeed quite satisfactory. Still, ability to correct for bias constitutes a tenuous sole justification for the preference for redundancy coefficients. The justification is particularly tenuous since the correction will primarily be needed with small sample sizes for which the central limit theorem cannot be invoked. Furthermore, Weinberg and Darlington (1976) have proposed an analog to canonical correlation analysis that may be used when bias is a concern and, according to the title of their article, "when number of variables is large relative to sample size."

In 1977 Wollenberg (p. 208) noted that "canonical correlation analysis only maximizes one part of the redundancy formula. It would seem reasonable, however, to try and maximize redundancy per se." He proposed an analytic technique that optimizes redundancy as against canonical correlation and termed the new technique "redundancy analysis." However, he noted that it is not, in general, possible to have *bi-orthogonal* components in redundancy analysis, i.e. the components in the one set are not necessarily orthogonal to the components in the other set, since, Xw and Yv [redundancy function coefficients] are determined separately (in canonical correlation analysis the canonical components are determined bi-orthogonally) [p. 210].

Johansson (1981: 100) noted that

the property of biorthogonality is without doubt very attractive. Not only does it make for a very elegant solution, but one can employ the derived variates knowing that they represent fundamentally distinct sources of variation in the underlying variables. For example, in canonical correlation where the variates are biorthogonal, the successive variates generated by the analysis can be properly viewed as representing variability not accounted for already.

Johansson then proposed an extension of redundancy analysis that does generate bi-orthogonal redundancy functions. DeSarbo (1981: 328) suggested that both canonical analysis and redundancy analysis have some attractive features:

As mentioned, canonical correlation renders maximally related linear composites which, however, may not be very much related to the original sets of variables. Conversely, redundancy maximization renders linear composites maximally related to the original sets of variables, but may be somewhat unrelated to each other.

DeSarbo then presented a technique that allows the researcher to declare how much relative weight should be given to optimizing redundancy or canonical correlation; he termed the technique "canonical/redundancy factoring."

In short, these various considerations suggest that the redundancy coefficients computed in a canonical analysis may have somewhat limited value. Thompson (1980a: 16) does present one possible use:

A redundancy coefficient can equal 1.0 only when two variates share exactly 100% of their variance (Rc = 1.0) and a variate perfectly represents the original variables in its domain, i.e.—all the squared structure coefficients for the domain equal 1.0. This suggests that redundancy coefficients can be interpreted as indices which assess how well intra-domain relationships are represented by g-variates and how well inter-domain relationships are represented by g-functions.

However, the statistic seems to make more sense in the context of redundancy analysis or some variant of redundancy analysis.

As to the relative merits of redundancy as opposed to canonical analysis, redundancy analysis makes the most sense when the researcher's primary interest is in deriving functions which "capture" variance in the original, unweighted variables, that is, when the primary concern is function "adequacy." Canonical correlation analysis will be the method of choice when the researcher is primarily interested in exploring relationships between the variable sets. It is interesting, though, to return to Stewart and Love's (1968: 163) published presentation of their index to consider the symbol they selected to represent the index and the position they took with respect to the statistic's possible use; they suggested that "the utility of $\bar{R}^2$ is as a summary index. In general it is not to be viewed as an analytic tool." Of course, this position was taken prior to the development of redundancy analysis techniques.

Index Coefficients

Coefficients labeled *index* coefficients by Thompson and Frankiewicz (1979) are also helpful albeit less controversial aids to interpretation. Like structure coefficients, index coefficients are also correlation coefficients. Table 7 provides a presentation of the statistic from a bivariate perspective. The matrix computations for some other hypothetical case involving three variables in set "1" and two variables in set "2" would be:

$$R11_{(3 \times 3)} \; W1_{(3 \times 2)} = S1_{(3 \times 2)}$$

$$R12_{(3 \times 2)} \; W2_{(2 \times 2)} = I1_{(3 \times 2)}$$

$$R22_{(2 \times 2)} \; W2_{(2 \times 2)} = S2_{(2 \times 2)}$$

$$R21_{(2 \times 3)} \; W1_{(3 \times 2)} = I2_{(2 \times 2)}$$

where R represents the various quadrants in the correlation matrix, W represents the "weight" or function coefficient matrices (which can only have two columns here since the smaller of the two variable sets only has two variables), and S and I, respectively, represent the canonical structure and index coefficient matrices. Index coefficients represent the correlation between scores on one original, unweighted (via function coefficients) variable and the weighted and aggregated original variables, i.e., variate scores, for the variables in the *other* variable set.

Kuylen and Verhallen (1981: 229) note that "the cross loadings [index coefficients] are more conservative, less inflated than within-set loadings [structure coefficients] and form a more solid base for interpretation." Thompson (1980b: 156) presents a substantive application of these coefficients:

> It was suggested at the outset of the study that both role ideals and philosophical beliefs should be related to preferences for models of teaching. The question now arises as to whether either the role-ideals or the philosophy variables accounted for a preponderant portion of the variance these variables shared with the models of teaching factors [i.e., the criterion variables]. This question can be addressed by squaring the Table 4 index coefficients, and then summing first the squares for the role-ideals variables and then the squares for the philosophy factors. A comparison of these four pairs of sums suggests that both sets of [predictor] variables shared roughly the same proportions of variance with the models of teaching factors.

Thus, Timm and Carlson (1976: 161) suggest that "the relationships between canonical variates in one set and individual variates in the other [index coefficients] should be examined in addition to the correlations within a set [structure coefficients] to better understand canonical variates."

4. SUPPLEMENTARY ANALYTIC TECHNIQUES

Function Rotation

The close family lineage between canonical correlation analysis and principal components analysis (Burt, 1948) has already been acknowledged. A brief discussion of rotation of principal components may facilitate subsequent consideration of rotation as an aid to the interpretation of canonical results. Factors are "extracted" from a correlation matrix (or some other matrix of association statistics) subject to the

TABLE 11
Matrix to Be Factored

	VAR1	VAR2	VAR3	VAR4
VAR1	1.0			
VAR2	.5	1.0		
VAR3	.2	.1	1.0	
VAR4	.0	−.1	.6	1.0

restriction that each factor must be unrelated to every other factor. Furthermore, at least conceptually the factors are extracted subject to a restriction that each factor will come as close as possible to reproducing the correlation matrix. Thus factors tend to each account for a decreasing amount of variance in the matrix from which the factors were derived. Thompson and Miller (1978: 57), for example, present a correlation matrix and what remained of the matrix after the extraction of four factors.

The requirement that each new factor must come as close as possible to reproducing the matrix from which it was extracted is an attractive feature because the procedure may yield a minority of all possible factors (i.e., the number of variables) that will reproduce a majority of the variance in the correlation matrix. However, this property makes interpretation of factors difficult since the mathematics mean that as many variables as possible will be correlated with each factor. Thus, the interpretation of the first principal component extracted from a correlation matrix tends to be very difficult indeed since each variable tends to be correlated with the factor.

Thurstone (1935) suggested that this problem could be overcome by "rotating" the factors toward "simple" structure. This sort of rotation is legitimate since it can be shown that a given subset of rotated factors and a corresponding set of unrotated factors will do exactly equally well at reproducing the matrix from which the factors were extracted. Furthermore, rotation does not alter the "position" of the variables relative to each other.

This can be illustrated by considering the hypothetical correlation matrix presented in Table 11. Table 12 presents the first two principal components extracted both before and after rotation. Both solutions will reproduce roughly 79 percent (3.144/4 = .7861) of the variance represented in the Table 11 correlation matrix. The rotation simply

TABLE 12
Principal Components

Variable	Unrotated			Rotated		
	I	II	h^2	I	II	h^2
VAR1	.58	.64	.75	.11	.86	.75
VAR2	.45	.74	.75	−.05	.87	.75
VAR3	.83	−.35	.82	.88	.18	.82
VAR4	.67	−.61	.83	.90	−.12	.83
Sum of Squares	1.68	1.47	3.14	1.61	1.54	3.14

NOTE: (.58x.58) + (.45x.45) + (.83x.83) + (.67x.67) = 1.68.
.75 + .75 + .82 + .83 = 1.68 + 1.47 = 3.14.

"reallocates" the variance across the factors so that the results are "simpler." Figure 2 demonstrates that rotation does not change the position in factor space of the variables relative to each other.

Thurstone (1947: 335) subsequently developed criteria for determining whether a rotation had maximized "simple" structure. One implication of the criteria is that a limited number of variables should be correlated with each factor. Kaiser (1956) eventually developed a method for this sort of rotation for his doctoral dissertation. His "varimax" rotation is the most widely used rotation strategy (Kaiser, 1970: 402). Kim (1975: 485) concurs, noting that "this method of rotation is the most widely used."

Given the close affinity between principal components analysis and canonical correlation analysis, it was logical that varimax rotation of canonical results would eventually be recommended. Of course, rotation is only possible when there are at least two functions. The required preservation of each variable's communality means that in the case of a single function, variance cannot be reallocated—the function's position is fixed.

In a seminal work Cliff and Krus (1976: 42) argued that

> rotation of the canonical variates [functions] does not seem to violate the properties of the method and the transformed variates appear to be more meaningful than the original ones. It seems therefore reasonable to recommend that the canonical weights [function coefficients] or structure correlations be routinely rotated orthogonally by the usual methods employed in factor analysis.

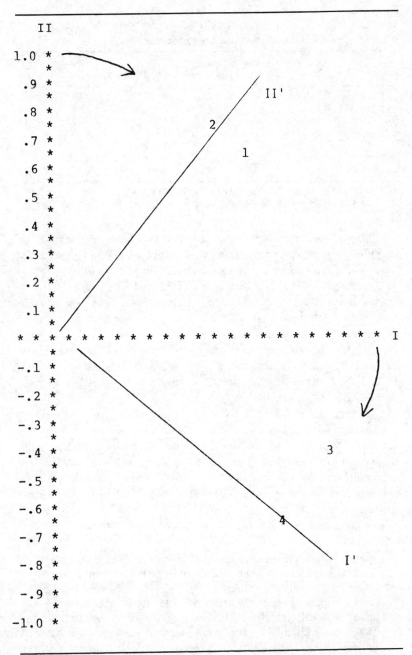

Figure 2: Variables in Factor Space

Most important, Cliff and Krus demonstrated that rotation, although it redistributes variance across functions, preserves the overall capacity of the solution to reproduce variance in the matrix, A, from which the functions were derived. That is, the sums of the squared canonical correlation coefficients for rotated and unrotated functions are equal.

It has also been suggested that varimax rotation yields results that are more replicable in future work. This property is termed "invariance." Kuylen and Verhallen (1981: 221) explain:

> In most cases, as for instance with varimax rotation, the rotation leads up to a simpler structure with better interpretable results. A second consequence of rotation is factorial invariance. This means that the results of a solution can be generalized. A solution is said to be invariant when the same groups of variables are found repeatedly on variates whenever at least some important variables, which reflect the underlying construct, are used in the repeated analysis.

Theoretically invariance is associated with simpler or more parsimonious results because, as William of Occam suggested centuries ago, the simplest solution is most often true and is thus most likely to reoccur. However, as Ping and Tucker (1976: 8) note:

> Actually the simple structure concept is based on the idea of parsimony. It is more of an ideal than a realizable objective. Empirical data have many dependencies that prohibit attaining ideal simple structure but the factors are best located when the produced structure is as simple as possible.

Of course, in a principal components analysis there is only one matrix available for rotation. In a canonical analysis several matrices could be rotated. For example, either the function or the structure coefficients could be rotated:

> Note that the assumption has been made that the correlation with the variates [structure coefficients] forms the basis for deciding on the transformation. This is felt to be a meaningful approach to interpretability but there is nothing in the mathematics to preclude directly rotating the configuration of the weights [function coefficients] [Cliff and Krus, 1976: 38].

Cliff and Krus seem to recommend rotation of the structure matrix and then present a rotation of canonical functions as an heuristic example.

Reynolds and Jackosfsky (1981: 667) make a convincing case for the rotation of the structure matrix:

> It should again be pointed out that the canonical weights [function coefficients] are analogous to regression betas and, thus, are not constrained to be less than one. This fact, in combination with the varimax criterion, tends to result in extreme solutions. Thus, the standardized nature of the structure coefficients [which as correlation coefficents can only vary between −1 and +1] becomes even more appealing when rotation for the sake of interpretability is considered.

However, an even more convincing case can be made.

As demonstrated in Table 12, rotation does preserve the sums of the squared coefficients computed for rows across columns. With respect to structure coefficients these values are communality coefficients. The sums of squared variate coefficients across columns have no such intrinsic psychometric meaning.

A demonstration of the rotation procedure may be helpful. Table 13 presents the correlation matrix for the study reported by Thompson (1980b). The study involved data on 10 predictor variables and four criterion variables collected from 235 subjects. Table 14 presents the function coefficients derived in the analysis. Table 15 presents the structure coefficient matrix for the solution. Table 16 presents the structure matrix after rotation to the varimax criterion; this rotation was performed using the widely available *Statistical Package for the Social Sciences* (SPSS).

After rotation the other canonical coefficients must be recomputed. The formulas in this case for computing the new function coefficients were:

$$R11^{-1}_{(10 \times 10)} \, S1^*_{(10 \times 4)} = W1^*_{(10 \times 4)}$$
$$R22^{-1}_{(4 \times 4)} \, S2^*_{(4 \times 4)} = W2^*_{(4 \times 4)}$$

where S^* and W^* refer, respectively, to the postrotation structure and function coefficients. Table 17 presents the new function coefficients. Incidentally, in this case S^* does exactly equal W^* for the second variable set because $R22$ is an identity matrix and because the inversion of an identity matrix also yields an identity matrix.

The canonical correlation coefficients also must be recomputed using the new function coefficients. Table 18 presents these values. As proven

TABLE 13
Correlation Matrix

Variables	Predictor Variables										Criterion Variables			
	1	2	3	4	5	6	7	8	9	10	1	2	3	4
Impotent		000	000	000	251	-061	-066	-079	037	011	154	179	-257	129
Rigorous	000		000	000	-010	074	-057	146	053	076	098	-090	063	222
Scholarly	000	000		000	-136	072	120	136	095	023	093	013	203	062
Warm	000	000	000		-137	-045	130	-138	051	-010	117	199	053	033
Existentialism	251	-010	-136	-137		000	000	000	001	000	122	161	-132	-102
Rationalism	-061	074	072	-045	000		000	000	000	000	043	-072	147	069
Progressivism	-066	-057	120	130	000	000		000	000	000	-039	146	261	087
Perennialism	-079	146	136	-138	000	000	000		000	000	101	-128	078	046
Humanism	037	053	095	051	001	000	000	000		000	-025	082	080	159
Essentialism	011	076	023	-010	000	000	000	000	000		171	-103	049	-151
Structured	154	098	093	117	122	043	-039	101	-025	171		000	000	000
Affective	179	-090	013	199	161	-072	146	-128	082	-103	000		000	000
Incisive	-257	063	203	053	-132	147	261	078	080	049	000	000		000
Inquiry	129	222	062	033	-102	069	087	046	159	-151	000	000	000	

NOTE: Decimals and diagonal entries omitted.

TABLE 14
Canonical Function Coefficients
(n = 235)

	I	II	III	IV
1	0.402	0.604	−0.170	0.380
2	−0.296	0.292	−0.142	0.524
3	−0.233	0.126	0.403	0.019
4	0.124	0.412	0.492	−0.113
5	0.353	0.126	0.502	−0.251
6	−0.290	0.033	0.134	0.187
7	−0.483	0.324	0.053	−0.407
8	−0.092	−0.034	0.208	0.397
9	−0.233	0.291	−0.196	−0.100
10	0.069	−0.323	0.616	0.242
1	0.181	0.285	0.747	0.573
2	0.246	0.698	0.173	−0.650
3	−0.873	−0.030	0.417	−0.251
4	−0.380	0.657	−0.489	0.431

NOTE: Variables listed in Table 13.

by Cliff and Krus (1976), the sums of the squared canonical correlation coefficients for both the rotated and the unrotated solutions are equal. The minimal deviation (.010) is due to rounding error from the several matrix computations involved in the calculations.

Although the varimax rotation is appealing, the application seriously violates the fundamental logic of a canonical analysis. Thorndike (1976a: 4) puts the matter quite clearly and conclusively:

> The two sets of variables presumably have been kept separate for a reason. If an investigator is interested in the structure of the combined sets, then he probably should have performed a traditional factor analysis in the first place.

Bentler and Huba (1982: 31) note that the varimax rotation of the structure matrix in many cases

> can be defended because one has no particular reason to be concerned with simplification in one matrix versus simplification in the other matrix. However, it must be recognized that this method implicitly weights each matrix in proportion to the number of variables in the set.... It could happen, in some examples, that all

TABLE 15
Canonical Structure Coefficients
($n = 235$)

	I	I	III	IV	h^2
1	0.540	0.622	-0.073	0.300	0.774
2	-0.314	0.261	-0.073	0.635	0.575
3	-0.393	0.166	0.374	0.067	0.327
4	0.026	0.458	0.379	-0.202	0.395
5	0.471	0.202	0.339	-0.149	0.399
6	-0.359	0.008	0.141	0.209	0.193
7	-0.505	0.336	0.185	-0.475	0.627
8	-0.216	-0.079	0.187	0.462	0.302
9	-0.250	0.362	-0.146	-0.062	0.219
10	0.044	-0.296	0.607	0.287	0.541
1	0.181	0.285	0.747	0.573	1.000
2	0.246	0.698	0.173	-0.650	1.000
3	-0.873	-0.030	0.417	-0.251	1.000
4	-0.380	0.657	-0.489	0.431	1.000

the simplification occurs in one set and virtually none in the other. Such a phenomenon is sometimes best left not to chance, but rather to the control of the experimenter.

Bentler and Huba (1982) propose a rotation procedure that seeks to simplify canonical results under the constraint that membership in variable sets must be honored and considered in deriving the transformation matrix, T. Furthermore, they propose (p. 32) a parameter, alpha ($0 < $ alpha < 1), that is chosen by the researcher and that "represents the relative influence one would like the X variables to have in the rotation. In the absence of a specific rationale, α should probably represent the proportion of variables in the X set so that each variable has approximately the same influence on the solution." However, in some cases, the researcher may well prefer to clarify the structure of one variable set at the expense of the other set. Huba, Palisoc, and Bentler (1982) present a computer program that calculates these rotations as well as other helpful interpretation aids.

Table 19 presents a rotation of the Table 15 structure matrix with the alpha parameter declared to be 10/14 or .7143. As before, the squared canonical coefficients (.178, .155, .109, .140) sum to .582.

In summary, rotating can be a useful adjunct to routine canonical analysis, particularly if the rotation considers membership in variable

TABLE 16
Varimax Rotated Structure

	I	II	III	IV	h^2
1	−0.585	0.141	0.515	0.383	0.774
2	−0.012	0.496	−0.186	0.543	0.576
3	0.444	0.326	0.123	0.090	0.327
4	0.210	0.074	0.585	0.056	0.395
5	−0.206	0.037	0.543	−0.248	0.400
6	0.269	0.291	−0.136	0.131	0.193
7	0.691	−0.201	0.286	0.170	0.629
8	0.062	0.500	−0.202	0.077	0.301
9	0.190	−0.104	0.106	0.401	0.219
10	0.063	0.584	0.010	−0.442	0.540
1	−0.101	0.887	0.447	−0.057	1.000
2	0.135	−0.425	0.889	0.106	1.000
3	0.985	0.152	−0.077	−0.003	0.999
4	−0.017	0.097	−0.069	0.993	1.001

sets. Still, rotation is not without its cost. First, as Carlson (1982: 11) notes,

> Rotation, of course, destroys some of the properties of the canonical solution (as is pointed out in the papers referred to above) notably the biorthogonal property of the variates to be interpreted. . . . That is, the matrix of correlations between the U_i and the V_i [two sets of variate scores] is no longer diagonal.

However, it is noteworthy that even for the solution associated with the varimax rotation reported in Tables 16 and 17 the *largest* correlation between variate scores for different functions involved the correlation ($r = -.0432$) between the variate scores for the predictor variate on function I and for the criterion variate on function IV. The coefficient of determination (.0019) suggests a problem of minimal magnitude. Second, Carlson (1982: 11) notes, "Furthermore, the maximal correlational property of the solution is destroyed, although the sum of common variance remains the same since this is dependent only on the magnitude of the projection of one vector space onto the other and not on the particular vectors chosen as basis vectors." Still, these difficulties may represent reasonable tradeoffs in favor of improved interpretability and possibly more invariant results. But Bentler and Huba's (1982: 42) admonition should be emphasized: "The form of rotation used should be consistent

TABLE 17
Function Coefficient for Rotated Structure

	I	II	III	IV
1	−0.538	0.160	0.374	0.495
2	−0.007	0.366	−0.154	0.558
3	0.339	0.286	0.188	−0.026
4	0.132	0.200	0.617	−0.040
5	−0.007	0.067	0.557	−0.376
6	0.218	0.262	−0.088	0.120
7	0.597	−0.230	0.199	0.242
8	−0.007	0.448	−0.091	0.033
9	0.172	−0.166	0.050	0.358
10	0.063	0.550	0.020	−0.490
1	−0.101	0.887	0.447	−0.057
2	0.135	−0.425	0.889	0.106
3	0.985	0.152	−0.077	−0.003
4	−0.017	0.097	−0.069	0.993

with major theories of the phenomenon. This point cannot be stressed too strongly."

Invariance Calculations

The tendency of correlation methods to capitalize on chance is widely recognized. As Nunnally (1967: 280) notes, "one tends to take advantage of chance in any situation where something is optimized from the data at hand." Thompson (1981b) has termed estimates of this capitalization *invariance coefficients*. Cross-validation procedures yielding invariance coefficients have been developed for a number of methods, including factor analysis (Gorsuch, 1974: 252) and multiple regression analysis (Huck, Cormier, and Bounds, 1974: p. 159).

Canonical correlation analysis tends particularly to capitalize on sampling error. As Fornell (1978: 76) notes:

Since they appear to make the long and mazy road of analysis much shorter, the multivariate methods are the racing machines or analysis. Like most sophisticated racing vehicles, they are extremely sensitive to chance variation, demanding a thorough understanding of their delicate machinery in order to give top performance and to avoid possible contretemps.

42

TABLE 18
Canonical Correlation Coefficients

	I	II	II	IV	Sum
Rc^2	.210	.176	.113	.094	.593
Rc^*	.174	.102	.154	.152	.583

NOTE: The first row of correlations is associated with the unrotated functions; the second row is associated with the varimax rotated results.

Thus Rader (1975: 57-58) suggests that

> in order to use the canonical correlations for prediction of an individual event, we need to be sure that the canonical correlation for our sample is a very close estimation of the canonical correlation of the entire population. To accomplish this, we can either cross-validate using the Beta weights [function coefficients], or repeat the canonical correlation using another sample from the same population. Cross-validation is used primarily where the form of the relationship is important, while replication is important when the concern is the amount of relationship.

Two invariance procedures have been recommended for use in canonical correlation analysis. Both procedures involve randomly splitting the data into two subgroups.

Thorndike (1978: 192) proposed the following method for computing canonical invariance coefficients: "The predictor and criterion standard [Z] scores of each individual in the cross-validation group are multiplied by the appropriate canonical weights for a pair of composites and summed to yield scores on the two composites. The product moment correlation between these composite scores is the cross-validation canonical correlation" or canonical invariance coefficient.

The Table 1 data can be employed to provide a heuristic demonstration of Thorndike's method. The cases were randomly assigned (see Table 20) to either subgroup Q (cases 1, 3, 4, 7 and 9) or subgroup R (cases 2, 5, 6, 8 and 10). Separate canonical analyses were then performed on both data subsets. In order to simplify this discussion, calculation of only one invariance coefficient for the first of the two possible canonical functions will be presented. Table 21 presents the canonical composites obtained by multiplying subgroup Q's Z scores by the canonical function coefficients derived by analyzing the subgroup Q

TABLE 19
Simultaneous Rotation of the Two Structures

	I	II	III	IV	h^2
1	−0.298	0.771	0.071	−0.292	0.774
2	0.115	0.475	0.208	0.542	0.576
3	0.474	0.037	0.304	0.086	0.326
4	0.355	0.232	0.177	−0.429	0.395
5	−0.129	0.119	0.231	−0.562	0.400
6	0.261	0.016	0.196	0.293	0.193
7	0.753	−0.049	−0.157	−0.184	0.628
8	0.042	0.073	0.384	0.383	0.301
9	0.317	0.266	−0.212	0.047	0.218
10	−0.056	−0.228	0.696	0.030	0.540
1	0.020	0.396	0.913	−0.098	1.000
2	0.364	0.307	−0.232	−0.848	1.000
3	0.894	−0.363	0.161	0.208	1.000
4	0.262	0.786	−0.295	0.477	1.001

data (Rc = .994). The table also presents the composites derived by multiplying subgroup Q's Z scores by the canonical function coefficients derived by independently analyzing subgroup R's data; the invariance coefficient derived in this manner was .305. This decrement from the previous value of .994 suggests that the data do not produce invariant results; the finding is not surprising since multivariate analyses involving 10 subjects and four variables should not be expected to be very invariant.

Actually, this one logic can be used to provide two possible estimates of invariance. As already exemplified in Table 21, the Rc for subgroup Q generated with subgroup Q's own function coefficients (.994) can be compared with the Rc for subgroup Q generated using subgroup R's function coefficients (.305). But a "double" cross-validation could be conducted by also comparing the Rc for subgroup R generated using subgroup R's function coefficients against the Rc for subgroup R generated using subgroup Q's function coefficients.

The close linkage between principal components analysis and canonical correlation analysis suggests a second logic for invariance estimation (Thompson, 1982b). Canonical results from two data subgroups could be rotated to a position of "best fit" using a computer program Veldman (1967) developed for use in factor analysis. Kaiser, Hunka, and Bianchini (1969) suggested that the cosines of the angles among the

TABLE 20
Cases Assigned to Random Subgroups

Case	X	Y	A	B
Subgroup Q				
1	1 (−0.61)	9 (+0.68)	4 (+0.09)	6 (+0.00)
3	3 (+0.92)	9 (+0.68)	6 (+0.96)	0 (−1.63)
4	3 (+0.92)	4 (−0.54)	6 (+0.96)	9 (+0.82)
7	2 (+0.15)	0 (−1.52)	2 (−0.79)	9 (+0.82)
9	0 (−1.38)	9 (+0.68)	1 (−1.23)	6 (+0.00)
Subgroup R				
2	5 (+1.43)	4 (+1.43)	0 (−0.73)	8 (+1.25)
5	3 (+0.33)	3 (+0.24)	9 (+1.10)	0 (−1.03)
6	2 (−0.22)	2 (−0.96)	9 (+1.10)	0 (−1.03)
8	0 (−1.32)	2 (−0.96)	0 (−0.73)	5 (+0.40)
10	2 (−0.22)	3 (+0.24)	0 (−0.73)	5 (+0.40)

NOTE: Z-score equivalents of the unstandardized data are presented in parentheses.

rotated factors (or other rotated structures) are correlation coefficients. The cosines calculated by the computer program in this application are invariance coefficients.

Table 22 provides a concrete example of this logic. The table was derived from data from a study (Pitts and Thompson, 1984) of cognitive styles and reading comprehension abilities. The sample ($n = 127$) was randomly divided roughly into halves and the two canonical solutions reported in the table were calculated independently. Solution "B" was then rotated to a position of best fit with Solution A in order to derive the cosines reported in Table 23. The selection of Solution "A" as the "target" solution for the Procrustean rotation was arbitrary since the procedure is primarily performed to produce the cosines and the cosines should be stable across selection of a solution to be the "target." However, some researchers prefer to identify a "hold-out" sample that represents much less than half of the sample. In such cases it might be appropriate to designate the solution associated with the larger sample subgroup as the "target" solution since, by virtue of a larger sample size, this solution should theoretically be more stable.

Thompson (1982b: 5) notes that

the difficulty with [varimax] rotation of canonical functions is that the rotation procedure ignores membership in variable sets, and so the rotated canonical function weights may no longer optimize the

TABLE 21
Invariance Cauculations

Case	ZX	F1	ZY	F2	Criterion Composite	Predictor Composite		ZA	F3	ZB	F4
					Composites Derived with Subgroup Q Function Coefficients						
1	(−0.61)	(F1) +	(+0.68)	(F2) =	−0.08	+0.07	=	(+0.09)	(F3) +	(+0.00)	(F4)
3	(+0.92)	(F1) +	(+0.68)	(F2) =	+1.43	+1.42	=	(+0.96)	(F3) +	(−1.63)	(F4)
4	(+0.92)	(F1) +	(−0.54)	(F2) =	+0.50	+0.41	=	(+0.96)	(F3) +	(+0.82)	(F4)
7	(+0.15)	(F1) +	(−1.52)	(F2) =	−1.00	−0.95	=	(−0.79)	(F3) +	(+0.82)	(F4)
9	(−1.38)	(F1) +	(+0.68)	(F2) =	−0.84	−0.95	=	(−1.23)	(F3) +	(+0.00)	(F4)
					Composites Derived with Subgroup R Function Coefficients						
1	(−0.61)	(F1) +	(+0.68)	(F2) =	−2.02	+0.25	=	(+0.09)	(F3) +	(+0.00)	(F4)
3	(+0.92)	(F1) +	(+0.68)	(F2) =	+0.92	−1.29	=	(+0.96)	(F3) +	(−1.63)	(F4)
4	(+0.92)	(F1) +	(−0.54)	(F2) =	+2.42	+4.72	=	(+0.96)	(F3) +	(+0.82)	(F4)
7	(+0.15)	(F1) +	(−1.52)	(F2) =	+2.16	−0.22	=	(−0.79)	(F3) +	(+0.82)	(F4)
9	(−1.38)	(F1) +	(+0.68)	(F2) =	−3.48	−3.46	=	(−1.23)	(F3) +	(+0.00)	(F4)

NOTE: The canonical function coefficients for subgroup Q are F1 = +0.98; F2 = +0.76; F3 = +0.78; F4 = −0.41. The canonical function coefficients for subgroup R are F1 = +1.92; F2 = −1.23; F3 = +2.81; F4 = +2.45.

canonical correlation. . . . [But] the "best fit" rotation presented as an invariance procedure does not violate the basic logic of canonical analysis, since the researcher will not be interested in interpreting the rotated canonical functions.

Incidentally, the structure coefficients can also be rotated to a "best fit" position. But the two rotation options do appear to address somewhat different questions. The rotation of functions investigates the similarity of function equations used to produce variate scores. The rotation of structures investigates similarity of the distribution of variable variances across equations. Unlike rotation for the purpose of clarifying solutions for interpretation purposes, both invariance rotation procedures seem plausible under certain conditions.

The relative merits of the various invariance estimates have yet to be clearly determined. The procedure discussed by Thorndike (1978) probably will tend to be somewhat conservative, particularly when the within-set correlations are nonzero and the across-set correlations are homogeneous. In these cases minor variations in the correlation matrices across solutions may generate fairly substantial variations in the

TABLE 22
Functions Rotated to Test Invariance

Variable	Solution A		Solution B		Solution B*	
	I	II	I	II	I	II
Ability on hard	.70	−1.11	.10	−1.34	.67	−1.17
Ability on easy	.40	1.25	.93	.97	.42	1.28
GEFT	−.17	.65	.17	1.09	−.32	1.06
Field independence	.78	.39	.68	−.52	.83	−.18
Grade level	.71	−.66	.57	−.33	.65	−.05

NOTE: Solution B* is Solution B rotated to a position of best fit with Solution A.

function coefficients, since the "weights" for highly correlated variables in a set do not capitalize on the same redundant variance and the sensitivity to redundant variance in variables may be relatively arbitrary and nongeneralizable. Of course, the rotation of the structure coefficient matrices would tend to avoid this difficulty.

However, the bias of the invariance procedures will also depend on the number of variables in the study. The rotational procedures will tend to become increasingly conservative as there are more variables since the positions of the rotated matrices will become more "determined" or fixed by more variables. But until the characteristics of the various invariance estimates are better known, it might be wise to employ several strategies to obtain both "lower bound" and "upper bound" estimates of the degree of capitalization on sampling specificity.

It is important to recognize that all procedures are "liberal" estimates of invariance when one data set is split into subgroups, because the two subgroups came from the same sample and the subgroups and their parameter estimates are therefore interdependent. A more conservative approach to the estimation of result invariance is provided when the canonical analysis involves two independent samples of subjects. For example, Thompson and Rucker (1980: 396) investigated canonical relationships involving students from two different community college campuses, and they only interpreted patterns that "occurred at both campuses; thus, some confidence can be vested in their replicability." This more conservative approach should be preferred whenever it can feasibly be implemented.

In any case, Tatsuoka's (1969: 28) admonition should be remembered:

TABLE 23
Cosines Among Function Axes

	I	II
Function I	.90	−.43
Function II	.43	.90

It should be pointed out that, necessary as the process of cross validation is, and reassuring as a favorable outcome from it may be, the latter should not lull us into a false sense of security. There is always the possibility that a change may occur in the population due to social, economic, cultural and other factors.

Still, invariance estimates are vitally important. Yet, in their review of over 30 applications of canonical analysis reported between 1965 and 1976, Wood and Erskine (1976) found only two studies that reported cross-validation. They concluded that "from this review of applications, it becomes apparent that many of the important methodological concerns in canonical analysis are either ignored or relegated to the incidental" (p. 864).

Backward Canonical Analysis

Thorndike (1978: 188) has argued that "as the number of variables increases, the probable effect of these sources of [error] variation on canonical correlations increases. Therefore, the fewer variables there are in a canonical analysis which yields a correlation of a given magnitude, the greater is the likelihood that that correlation is due to real, population-wide sources of covariation, rather than to sample-specific sources." This logic suggests that stepwise canonical correlation analysis should lessen the probability of inferential errors during hypothesis testing. Thompson (1982d: 881) has argued that a stepwise canonical analysis would also generally "provide more insight into the dynamics of social science phenomena."

Rim (1972: 22-25) proposed seven possible strategies for variable-reduction in a canonical analysis. For the purist, these strategies are backward variable elimination methods rather than stepwise procedures, since at each step of the analysis the strategies do not consider both possible elimination and possible inclusion of variables. For a variety of reasons (see Rim, 1972: 25), Rim elected to investigate in an empirical manner only two of the strategies.

> In one of the procedures, the normalized eigenvectors associated with the largest eigenvalue (square of the largest canonical correlation) were used as a selection index of a variable to be deleted at each step of the stepwise variable-elimination procedure. The sum of absolute products of significant eigenvalues and their associated eigenvectors was the other selection index; the variable that had the smallest sum was eliminated at each step of the variable-deletion procedure [p. 119].

Rim expected that the procedures would result in more parsimonious solutions that consequently would be more invariant and generalizable. As expected, he found that "the weights of the retained variables did not change much after the deletion of less contributing variables" (p. 124). Furthermore, Rim (1972: 124) found "that the use of reduced sets of variables brought about less shrinkage than the use of the whole sets of variables." Long (1974) subsequently proposed that redundancy coefficients might be used instead of squared canonical correlation coefficients (eigenvalues) as weights in deriving selection indices.

Several problems with these various possibilities can be noted. The sole use of the first of many possible eigenvalues seems to violate the fundamental logic of multivariate analysis. The use of function coefficients rather than structure coefficients seems inappropriate, for the same reasons that structure coefficients seem to be more appropriate coefficients to consult in interpretation. The use of redundancy coefficients in a multivariate analysis in which these nonmultivariate statistics are not optimized also seems inappropriate.

Thompson (1982d, 1982e) has proposed a more straightforward logic for performing backward canonical correlation analysis. Data reported by Pitts and Thompson (1984) provide a concrete basis for this discussion. The theoretical framework for the study can be derived from that report; it will be noted here only that the study involved two criterion variables and five predictor variables.

Table 24 presents the canonical results from the first step of the analysis. The last column of Table 24 presents what Thompson (1980a: 19) has termed "canonical communality coefficients." As noted previously, a squared canonical structure coefficient indicates how much variance a variable linearly shares with a canonical variate. Since canon-

TABLE 24
Canonical Solution for First Step
(n = 127)

Variable	Function I			Function II			h^2
	F	S	SSQ	F	S	SSQ	
Ability on hard	.43	.87	.75	−1.26	−.50	.25	1.00
Ability on easy	.66	.95	.89	1.16	.33	.11	1.00
GEFT	−.10	.39	.15	1.02	.83	.70	.84
Field independence	.69	.71	.51	.00	.32	.10	.61
Attentional style	−.34	−.36	.13	.31	.16	.03	.16
Reflective impulsive	.26	.41	.17	.02	.06	.00	.18
Grade level	.53	.60	.36	−.49	−.20	.04	.39

NOTE: F = canonical function coefficients; S = canonical structure coefficients; SSQ = squared canonical structure coefficients; h^2 = canonical communality coefficients.

ical functions are orthogonal or uncorrelated, the sum of a variable's squared canonical structure coefficients across all possible functions indicates how much of the variable's variance can be reproduced from the complete canonical solution. Or, viewed differently, a canonical communality coefficient indicates both how much a variable contributed to the overall solution and how much the solution would be altered by the deletion of the variable.

In this case, the Table 24 results suggested that the attentional style predictor variable had a disproportionately low canonical communality coefficient. Consequently, this variable was deleted during the second step of backward analysis, and the canonical analysis was repeated. Since the reflective impulsive predictor variable continued to have a disproportionately low communality coefficient (.19), this variable was also deleted and a third step of analysis was performed. The results of the third step of analysis are presented in Table 25. Stepwise analysis was terminated at this step since the communality coefficients at this step were reasonably homogeneous.

For those with a penchant for statistical significance tests, Rim (1972: 27) has proposed a stopping rule to determine when variable elimination should be terminated. The formula is:

$$\frac{chi^2(pq) - chi^2(p'q')/(pq - p'q')}{chi^2(p'q')/(p'q')}$$

TABLE 25
Final Canonical Solution ($n = 127$)

Variable	Function I				Function II				h^2
	F	I	S	SSQ	F	I	S	SSQ	
Ability on hard	.38	.53	.85	.72	−1.27	−.10	−.53	.28	1.00
Ability on easy	.70	.60	.96	.92	1.13	.06	.29	.08	1.00
GEFT	.00	.28	.44	.19	1.02	.16	.82	.68	.87
Field Independence	.76	.50	.79	.63	−.08	.05	.24	.06	.68
Grade level	.61	.41	.66	.43	−.59	−.06	−.29	.09	.52

NOTE: F = canonical function coefficients; I = canonical index coefficients; S = canonical structure coefficients; SSQ = squared canonical structure coefficients; h^2 = canonical communality coefficients.

where pq represents the degrees of freedom associated with the chi-square involving the larger variable set and $p'q'$ represents the degrees of freedom for the smaller variable set consisting of either $(p - 1)$ predictors or $(q - 1)$ criterion variables. The value calculated with the formula is distributed as an F statistic with $(pq - p'q')$ and $(p'q')$ degrees of freedom.

Several possible variations on the backward elimination procedure can be noted. For example, the squared structure coefficients of each variable on each function might be multiplied by the squared canonical correlation coefficient for each function. Another variation would restrict variable elimination to only one of the two variable sets, for instance, requiring that only predictor variables may be eliminated from the analysis. Thompson (1982a) provides a computer program that performs this analysis and allows the user to make all variables eligible for elimination, or to restrict elimination to either of the two variable sets.

However, with all the variations on the basic technique it is particularly important to investigate the invariance of elimination decisions. Relatively minor fluctuations in parameter estimates could sometimes radically alter decisions regarding which variable should be eliminated at each step. But it must be emphasized that this problem will be dramatically less common in canonical analysis than in the regression case. Stepwise decisions in regression are typically based on partial correlation coefficients; these evaluations mean that one variable might be favored over another on the basis of infintesimally better predictive power that is redundant in another predictor variable. However, the decisions in the canonical procedure are a function of summated, squared structure coefficients; one of two variables might have a much larger function coefficient in such a situation but both variables would have comparable structure coefficients. Structure coefficients, unlike beta weights and partial correlation coefficients, are not "suppressed" by correlation with other variables in the same variable set. Of course, this is one reason that interpretation of structure coefficients is usually more helpful than interpretation of function coefficients, as noted previously.

The stepwise analog recommended here should accrue several advantages. First, the more parsimonious results should be more invariant or generalizable, as both theory and Rim's (1972) empirical results suggest. Second, the procedure may lessen Type II error probability by conserving degrees of freedom. For example, the degrees of freedom for the omnibus chi-square test statistic for a study involving five predictor variables and five criterion variables would be 25. The degrees of freedom after the removal of one variable from one of the two variable sets would be 20. Third, the procedure has heuristic value since it draws conceptual linkages with the more frequently applied stepwise or backward elimination multiple regression techniques. The linkage may make canonical analysis more understandable to some researchers. The linkage also reinforces the notion that all parametric techniques fall within the general linear model rubric as special cases of canonical analysis.

Some Canonical Extensions

Several variations on canonical methods have been proposed over the years. For example, Weinberg and Darlington (1976) proposed methods to be used when the research involves many subjects relative to variables. Meredith (1964) proposed methods that consider the fallibility of the data. Horst (1961) proposed methods that can be employed with more than two variable sets; Jain (1972) reports a computer program that automates this analysis and Tate (1982) provides an example substantive application of the technique. Although these three extensions are noteworthy, two other extensions will be discussed in more detail using concrete examples.

A number of researchers (e.g., Lee, 1978) have suggested that prior to computation of the matrix, A, the correlation matrix might be residualized for the influence of some other variable, set of variables, or even some third set of canonical variate scores. This analysis is an analog of the covariance procedures favored in some "OVA" applications. Table 26 presents a hypothetical correlation matrix which illustrates the procedure; the covariate, variable C, was employed to compute the

TABLE 26
Hypothetical Correlation Matrix

	X	Y	Z	A	B	C
X		.424	.545	−.025	−.264	−
Y	.469		.573	−.130	−.714	−
Z	.248	.470		−.002	−.487	−
A	.222	−.024	−.114		.164	−
B	−.176	−.680	−.482	.173		−
C	.602	.232	−.282	.398	.057	

NOTE: Simple bivariate correlation coefficients are presented below the diagonal; residualized correlation coefficients are presented above the diagonal.

partial correlations also reported in the table. Table 27 presents the function coefficients derived from canonical analysis of both the correlation matrices reported in Table 26.

However, just as application of covariance procedures in an analysis of variance can cause serious unrecognized problems (Campbell and Erlebacher, 1975), these procedures can also be problematic when applied in the canonical case as well. For example, Timm and Carlson (1976: 175) suggest that

> the difficulties encountered in using the variants of canonical correlation developed are not statistical, but pragmatic. The interpretation of partial, part, and bipartial canonical correlations are far from clear when variates are "partialled out" of variates they do not directly influence.

In short, the application presumes covariates that are very well understood and very reliable.

A second extension of canonical methods involves confirmatory rotation. Fornell (1982: 217) presents a case for use of the logic:

> An important consequence of Cliff and Krus's work is that it opens the door to using canonical analysis in a more confirmatory context. Since orthogonal rotation does not alter the fundamental properties of the canonical solution, it is possible to use confirmatory Procrustes rotation. Here, an a priori target matrix is formulated and the initial cononical solution is rotated toward this matrix. Although to my knowledge there have been no applications of this type of confirmatory canonical analysis, Procrustes methods of factor analysis have been discussed in psychometric texts.

TABLE 27
Canonical Functions

	Conventional		Partial	
	I	II	I	II
X	.256	1.016	.148	−.192
Y	−.922	.015	−.917	−.801
Z	−.295	−.403	−.226	1.278
A	−.018	1.015	−.004	1.014
B	1.003	−.158	1.001	−.163
Rc^2	.5245	.0750	.5260	.0117

Table 28 presents an heuristic application of the technique using the structure coefficients presented in Table 19 and Veldman's (1967) "best fit" rotation program.

However, Gorsuch (1974: 252) has recommended that the cosines of the angles among the *variables* must be consulted prior to interpretation of the cosines involving the *functions*, because "if the mean [variable] cosine is low, it is not possible to relate factors [or functions] at all since the relationships among the variables are different." For these data the mean cosine was .709 (SD = .386). However, the hypothetical target matrix included three variables that were presumed to have had no influence on the solution; it may be unusual to include variables in an analysis when one does not believe the variables will make a contribution to the solution. Excluding these outlying cosines for these three variables the mean cosine for the remaining 11 variables was .902 (SD = .046). The four cosines among the four functions across the actual and the "target" solutions were each greater than .98. This value suggests a close correspondence between expected and obtained results. It is important to emphasize that an actual research application of this procedure should involve a theory-based, a priori derivation of the target matrix. Furthermore, the logic of canonical analysis would seem to require that each variable set should have at least one substantial entry in the target matrix for each function. Wood and Erskine's (1976: 869) discussion of canonical interpretation makes the point:

> The ultimate label for a dimension should reflect a "higher-order" construct incapable of emerging from either set taken alone. It may well be, as implied above, that one variate is the more stable of the pair. . . . However, the very act of dimensional pursuit attests to

TABLE 28
"Best Fit" Structure Matrix

	I		II		III		IV	
1	−.32	(+0.0)	.68	(+1.0)	.13	(+0.0)	−.43	(+0.0)
2	.13	(+0.0)	.57	(+0.7)	.20	(+0.0)	.43	(+0.7)
3	.51	(+1.0)	.07	(+0.0)	.23	(+0.0)	.06	(+0.0)
4	.36	(+0.7)	.15	(+0.0)	.13	(+0.0)	−.48	(−0.7)
5	−.11	(+0.0)	.00	(+0.0)	.25	(+0.0)	−.57	(−1.0)
6	.29	(+0.0)	.08	(+0.0)	.16	(+0.0)	.28	(+0.0)
7	.72	(+1.0)	−.05	(+0.0)	−.27	(+0.0)	−.19	(+0.0)
8	.10	(+0.0)	.14	(+0.0)	.38	(+0.0)	.36	(+0.0)
9	.27	(+0.0)	.29	(+0.0)	−.25	(+0.0)	−.01	(+0.0)
10	.06	(+0.0)	−.23	(+0.0)	.69	(+1.0)	.08	(+0.0)
1	.14	(+0.0)	.35	(+0.0)	.91	(+1.0)	−.18	(+0.0)
2	.30	(+0.0)	.15	(+0.0)	−.28	(+0.0)	−.90	(−1.0)
3	.93	(+1.0)	−.28	(+0.0)	.02	(+0.0)	.25	(+0.0)
4	.19	(+0.0)	.88	(+1.0)	−.31	(+0.0)	.30	(+0.0)

NOTE: Rotated structure coefficients are *not* in parentheses; "target" matrix structure coefficients are in parentheses.

the presence of acceptable stability for *both* variates and thus cognizance of variables from both sets is demanded even though partiality toward one set may be justified.

5. SYNTHESIS AND SUMMARY

Rationale for the Multivariate General Linear Model

As noted earlier, canonical correlation analysis is the most general case for which all other parametric techniques represent special cases. These identities will not be discussed further, except to note that the general linear model techniques are exact analogs to ANOVA methods when all independent variables are nominally scaled. Thus, for example, Zinkgraf (1983) explained how researchers could compute MANOVA significance tests for balanced factorial designs using output from computer programs for conducting canonical correlation analysis.

In this regard it is important to emphasize that most variables, with the exception of sex and assignment to experimental conditions, are higher than nominally scaled. Furthermore, especially since Cronbach's (1957) presidential address to the American Psychological Association, researchers have increasingly included intervally scaled "aptitude" variables even in their experimental designs. These trends mean that most research situations involve data sets for which the general linear model techniques will produce different results than will their ANOVA analogs *unless the researcher converts the intervally scaled variables into nominal scale.* The costs of this conversion have been underrecognized in contemporary analytic practice and warrant serious consideration.

Ironically, the conversion distorts the model of the reality to which the researcher is purportedly trying to generalize. For example, consider the aptitude-treatment interaction design of an unnamed dissertation student who converted IQ into a trichotomy. Persons with IQs ranging from 61 to 76 inclusive were considered to have "low" IQs; persons with IQs ranging from 77 to 94 inclusive were considered to have "moderate" IQs; persons with IQs ranging from 95 to 108 inclusive were considered to have "high" IQs. Is intelligence in reality normally distributed with quasi-interval scale, or is the variable trichotomously distributed with equal numbers of persons in each of the three nominal categories? As Thompson (1981a: 8) observes, the assumption that the high IQ person with an IQ of 95 is equally as smart as the person with an IQ of 108 "seems untenable, even if the test's standard error of measurement was absurdly bad." Similarly, it seems unreasonable to consider the person with an IQ of 94 as being different from the person with an IQ of 95. As Cohen (1968: 441) notes, "this willful degradation of available measurement information has a direct consequence in the loss of statistical power." In summary, this practice squanders available information, distorts the variable by converting a normally distributed variable into a uniformly distributed variable, and distorts the variable's relationships with other independent variables by forcing the variable in Procrustean fashion to be perfectly uncorrelated with other variables with which the variable actually is related.

Cohen (1968: 440) argued that the cause of the overuse of ANOVA analogs lies partly "in their efficiency and computational simplicity." However, these advantages have been ameliorated by the increased availability of computer programs that rapidly and accurately perform even the most complicated calculations involved in implementing the multivariate general linear model. Unfortunately, the more serious barrier to the use of the multivariate general linear model is more impervious to change—too many researchers confuse the consequences of their *design* choices with the consequences of their *analytic* choices.

Researchers tend to prefer experimental designs over nonexperimental designs because, as even the most neophyte researchers know, experimental designs provide more complete information about causal relationships. As Thompson (1981a: 5) notes, "OVA procedures are very appropriate techniques with which to analyze data derived from experimental designs, because the experimental conditions by their nature tend to be nominally scaled, and because the dependent variables when subjects are people tend to approximate interval level of scale." However, this coincidence may have caused some researchers to associate "OVA" analyses with experimental designs. Yet it is the design *and not the analytic technique* that allows causal inferencing. Hicks (1973) provides a classic example of this confusion in his fine book, *Fundamental Concepts in the Design of Experiments*. The book is entirely about ANOVA techniques and does not touch at all upon experimental design issues.

It is important for social scientists to remember that both experimental and correlational studies are concerned with "the job of stating and testing more or less general relationships between properties of nature" (Homans, 1967: 7). The truth that all studies investigate relationship has been unconsciously recognized in the recent trend toward the computation of "effect sizes" even in experimental studies. Examples of these estimates include Hays's (1963: 382) omega squared and its multivariate analog. An increased emphasis on effect size estimates of relationship even in experimental studies is also reflected in the recently developed empirical techniques for synthesizing results across studies, that is, meta-analysis (Glass, McGaw, and Smith, 1981). Finally, researchers have increasingly emphasized effect size estimates even in experimental studies in recognition of the fact that statistically significant findings may not be psychologically or educationally significant (Carver, 1978). One hopes these trends will compel some researchers to develop more considered differentiations of designs and analytic techniques.

Given a preference for general linear model techniques, why should canonical analysis be preferred over factor analysis or multiple regression? With respect to factor analysis Wimmer (1977: 212) notes:

> One suggestion has been to perform two independent factor analysis of each variable set, then correlate the corresponding factor structures. . . . Independent factor analyses are fine if the researcher wants factors chosen independently of each other. It is not a good procedure if one wants to explain as much as possible of one set from the other set.

With respect to separate regression analyses Kuylen and Verhallen (1981: 225) note that "separate multiple regression analyses for each of the criterion variables would neglect the interrelations of the criteria." As Tatsuoka (1973: 273) explains,

> The often-heard argument, "I'm more interested in seeing how each variable, in its own right, affects the outcome" overlooks the fact that any variable taken in isolation may affect the criterion differently from the way it will act in the company of other variables. It also overlooks the fact that multivariate analysis— precisely by considering all the variables simultaneously—can throw light on how each one contributes to the relation.

Furthermore, significance testing of several different parameter estimates in a single experiment results in an inflated experimentwise Type I error probability; the degree of inflation is a function of the degree of correlation among the criterion variables (e.g., Morrow and Frankiewicz, 1979: 299).

The researcher's view of reality should also partially determine the selection of analytic techniques. As Wilkinson (1977: 487) notes,

> Variables which are meaningful taken alone rather than in linear combinations (e.g. physical measurements, molar behaviors) lend themselves to the individual response method. . . . When variables are meaningfully taken in linear combinations, however, the response variates approach is more appropriate. Test items, subscales of inventories, and behavioral measures of psychological traits all may qualify. Response variate analysis should be considered whenever a theory depends on profiles of responses rather than on responses taken separately.

Similarly, Kuylen and Verhallen (1981: 228) suggest that "we may want to incorporate more criterion variables because reality is complex and we hope that a composite criterion variate may better reflect reality than single criterion variables in separate regression analyses."

Limits and Uses of Canonical Analysis

Certainly there are numerous analytic techniques available to the researcher, and each has its own limits and uses. Thus canonical analysis has its limits. As suggested throughout this discussion, canonical analysis investigates relationships among at least two variable sets. The analysis does not inherently emphasize any one set of variables. As Tatsuoka (1973: 279) notes, "Actually, the choice of which set of variables to designate as 'predictors' and which as 'criteria' is [mathemati-cally] arbitrary. The analysis is symmetric with respect to the two sets."

The symmetric features of the method may be inappropriate if the researcher is primarily interested in predicting or explaining only one variable set. As Gulliksen (1968: 540) suggests,

> There is no particular interest in determining a criterion simply because one is able to predict it. Such a procedure would be subject to the rather extreme hazard that, for example, if there happened to be, say, a verbal test included in the criterion and a verbal test included in the predictors, then one would reach the conclusion that giving a very heavy weight to these two verbal tests would be the way to establish a "most predictable criterion" which would be quite unimportant for any practical purposes.

Cronbach (1971: 490) suggests that this feature of canonical analysis is particularly inappropriate in selection research:

> A canonical analysis will rearrange the criterion dimensions into . . . . whatever combination of outcomes is best predicted by the test data. An aspect of performance that is relatively easy to predict (e.g., likeability) will receive heavy weight in the canonical variate even though it interests the decision maker less than, say, the ability to solve problems creatively. In selection research, one must continually resist the temptation to focus on criteria that are easy to predict. Attention should go to those [criterion variables] that are most important.

Of course, canonical analysis need not be purely symmetric in all its aspects. For example, only predictor variables might be eliminated during backward variable elimination. Or the researcher might give greater weight to the criterion variable set when determining rotations. Still, canonical analysis may not be the most appropriate analytic technique in these applications. But there are so many research situations involving multiple predictors and multiple criteria that canonical analysis remains a very potent analytic technique, notwithstanding its limitations.

An initial step in the analytic process involves deriving "weights" or canonical function coefficients for the variables subject to the restriction that the linear relationships between the composites of the weighted variables across the variable sets will be optimized. In other words, no coefficients can possibly be found. Once calculated, these and the other

TABLE 29
Coefficients Used to Address Various Research Questions

Pooled Rc^2 or Pooled Rd	To what extent can one set of two or more variable be predicted or "explained" by another set of two or more variables?
Individual or pooled squared structure coefficient	What contribution does a single variable make to the explanatory power of the set of variables to which the variable belongs?
Individual or pooled squared index coefficient	To what extent does a single variable contribute to predicting or "explaining" the composite of the variables in the variable set to which the variable does not belong?
Structure coefficients for one function versus another	What different dynamics are involved in the ability of one variable set to "explain" in different ways different portions of the other variable set?
Rc^2 or Rd	What relative power do different canonical functions have to predict or explain relationships?
Invariance coefficients	How stable are canonical results across samples or sample subgroups?
Confirmatory rotation cosines	How closely do obtained canonical results conform to expected canonical results?

NOTE: Rd is already in the same metric as a squared canonical correlation coefficient, since Rd equals the variate adequacy coefficient for a set of variables (sum of the squared structure coefficients divided by the number of variables in the set) times the squared Rc for the function.

coefficients discussed previously can then be consulted for purposes of substantive interpretation.

Table 29 summarizes some of the questions that can be posed and identifies which results may be consulted to address these questions. In order to make discussion of these interpretation issues more concrete, the results reported by Thompson (1980b) will be employed as a heuristic. Perhaps the best way to understand a complex analytic technique is to iterate back and forth among conceptualizing the technique, implementing the technique, and practicing interpretation of results. Thus the Table 13 correlation matrix affords the reader a potentially helpful opportunity to replicate these results. Since rotation procedures are not yet widely available in statistical packages that implement canonical correlation analysis, somewhat arbitrarily, only the unrotated results will be discussed here. The same coefficients would be consulted in interpreting a rotated solution, but the numerical values for the various coefficients would themselves obviously tend to be somewhat different.

The most general question that can be posed in interpreting canonical results is, "To what extent can one set of two or more variables be predicted or explained by another set of two or more variables?" As noted in Table 29, the question can be approached from different vantage points by interpreting either a "pooled" Rc squared or Rd. Since canonical functions are uncorrelated or "orthogonal," the sum of all possible squared canonical correlation coefficients for a solution—that is, the "pooled" value—can range only between 0 and the number of variables in the smaller variable set. This is a useful interpretation feature, as indicated by the preference most social scientists have for interpreting bivariate correlation coefficients rather than their un-bounded counterparts, covariances. As reported in Table 18, the four sets of canonical variate scores share a total of 59.3 percent of their variance with each other. Put differently, the optimally *weighted* variables share 59.3 percent of their variance.

Redundancy coefficients indicate how well one set of variables can be reproduced from or explained by the other variable set. A pooled redundancy coefficient equals the sum of all possible Rds for a variable set. For example, the pooled redundancy coefficient for the criterion variable set in this case was .148 (.053 + .044 + .028 + .023). This result might be interpreted as indicating that the criterion variable set is not very well predicted by the predictor variables. However, as indicated by the communality coefficients reported in Table 15, 100 percent of all four variables is "captured" by the solution. As suggested previously, Rd actually indicates that the results are not characterized by one single function involving a substantial Rc and large structure coefficients for all the variables in the set, that is, a large variate adequacy coefficient. The result would be distressing only if such an outcome were theoretically expected.

The second question asks, "What contribution does a single variable make to the explanatory power of the set of variables to which the variable belongs?" This question can be addressed by considering either squared structure coefficients or canonical communality coefficients. For example, with respect to the results presented in Table 15, the communality coefficients suggest the predictor variable, "Impotent" (referring to beliefs about whether good teachers are simple, docile, and undirected) contains a substantial proportion (77.4 percent) of the predictive information represented in the four "weighted" sets of predictor variables. In terms of canonical functions taken one at a time, the squared structure coefficient indicates that this variable shares 29.1 percent (.540 × .540) of its variance with the predictor variate scores for the first canonical function. For example, the squared structure coefficients also suggest that the first predictor variate consists largely of the variables, "Impotent," "Progressivism," and "Warm" (referring to beliefs about the extent to which good teachers are warm, caring, and concerned). Among other uses, communality and structure coefficients can be consulted to determine which variables contribute the most to defining a solution and to determine the contribution of a variable to a given function.

The third question asks, "To what extent does a single variable contribute to predicting or explaining the composite of the variables in the variable set to which the variable does not belong?" This question can be addressed by considering either squared index coefficients or pooled squared index coefficients. Although not reported here (see Thompson, 1980b), the criterion variable with the largest index coefficient (–.401) was the variable, "Incisive" (referring to teachers' preferences to employ methods that emphasize fostering incisive understanding of a discipline's core concepts). A substantive application of these coefficients was presented previously when index coefficients were initially defined.

The fourth question asks, "What different dynamics are involved in the ability of one variable set to explain in different ways different portions of the other variable set?" This question can be addressed by interpreting canonical results in the same manner that orthogonal results from factor analysis are interpreted. Usually structure coefficients are interpreted for this purpose. For example, the Table 15 structure coefficients for the third canonical function have a connotation not unlike that associated with a "traditional" basic skills viewpoint. The function captures a dynamic involving preference for teaching methods that are highly structured, adherence to a philosophy of "Essentialism," preference for teaching methods that emphasize incisive inquiry, and a tendency to avoid teaching methods that are inquiry-oriented.

The fifth question asks, "What relative power do different canonical functions have to predict or explain relationships?" This question can be addressed by interpreting either squared canonical correlation coefficients or redundancy coefficients. For these results, for example, the squared canonical correlation coefficients (or eigenvalues) suggest that the first two sets of weighted variables share substantially more variance than does the fourth set of variate scores (21.0 percent versus 9.4 percent). This result suggests that the first function is the most helpful in interpreting relationships across the two variable sets.

The sixth question asks, "How stable are canonical results across samples or sample subgroups?" Invariance coefficients are consulted to address this question. Invariance analyses were not reported here for the data set summarized in the Table 13 correlation matrix. However, example interpretations were offered for the results presented in Tables 20 through 23.

The seventh question asks, "How closely do obtained canonical results conform to expected canonical results?" Confirmatory rotation cosines can be consulted to address this question. Table 28 presents an example application. As noted previously, the four cosines were each greater than .98. Since the cosines are treated as correlation coefficients, these values indicate that the "actual" and the "expected" results conformed quite closely. Of course, this result is an artifact of pretending to have expected a "target" solution that was quite similar to actual results.

Summary

Quality of research is generally a direct function of the researcher's dedication to careful, reflective decision making during all phases of an investigation, including the data analysis phase. Although it may be true that a study with a considered grounding in theory and good design may merit attention despite a less than fully appropriate analysis, it is nevertheless important that all phases of an investigation be as considered as possible. Of course, studies which are poorly conceptualized from an analysis standpoint may tend to be poorly conceptualized in other respects as well.

It has been suggested here that a more considered selection of analytic techniques would result in more frequent use of the multivariate general linear model—canonical correlation analysis. The technique has been underutilized in the past, partly because canonical computations have traditionally been presented in terms of abstract matrix algorithms. The various canonical coefficients were presented here as bivariate calculations; these are equally correct but are more intuitively straightforward.

It has also been suggested that researchers should be more hesitant to convert variables to nominal level of scale merely so that they can implement ANOVA techniques. This tendency has flourished primarily because some researchers confuse the consequences of design decisions with the consequences of analysis decisions.

A new method for stepwise variable reduction has been presented. Two methods of estimating the degree of solution capitalization on sampling error have been summarized. These invariance estimates are important whenever correlational methods are employed because these methods, and in particular stepwise methods, tend to capitalize on chance. Finally, it has been suggested that canonical correlation analysis may be more useful than redundancy analysis, although the latter technique does have some useful applications.

REFERENCES

ALLEN, M. J. and W. M. YEN (1979) Introduction to Measurement Theory. Monterey, CA: Brooks/Cole.

BAGGALEY, A. R. (1981) "Multivariate analysis: An introduction for consumers of behavioral research." Evaluation Review 5: 123-131.

BALON, R. E. and J. C. PHILPORT (1977) "Canonical correlation in mass communication research." Journal of Organizational Behavior 21: 199-209.

BARCIKOWSKI, R. S. and J. P. STEVENS (1975) "A Monte Carlo study of the stability of canonical correlations, canonical weights and canonical variate-variable correlations." Multivariate Behavioral Research 10: 353-364.

BARTLETT, M. S. (1948) "Internal and external factor analysis." British Journal of Psychology: Statistical Section 1: 73-81.

——— (1941) "The statistical significance of canonical correlations." Biometrika 32: 29-38.

BENTLER, P. M. and G. J. HUBA (1982) "Symmetric and asymmetric rotations in canonical correlation analysis: New methods with drug variable examples," in N. Hirschberg and L. G. Humphreys (eds.) Multivariate Applications in the Social Sciences. Hillsdale, NJ: Erlbaum.

BURT, C. (1948) "Factor analysis and canonical correlation." British Journal of Psychology 1: 96-106.

CAMPBELL, D. T. and A. ERLBACHER (1975) "How regression artifacts in quasi-experimental evaluations can mistakenly make compensatory education look harmful," in M. Guttentag and E. L. Struening (eds.) Handbook of Evaluation Research (vol. 1). Beverly Hills, CA: Sage.

CARLSON, J. E. (1982) "Use and interpretation of canonical analyses." Presented at the annual meeting of the American Educational Research Association, New York.

CARVER, R. P. (1978) "The case against statistical significance testing." Harvard Educational Review 48: 378-399.

CLIFF, N. and D. J. KRUS (1976) "Interpretation of canonical analysis: Rotated vs. unrotated solutions." Psychometrika 41: 35-42.

COHEN, J. (1968) "Multiple regression as a general data-analytic system." Psychological Bulletin 70: 426-443.

COOLEY, W. W. and P. R. LOHNES (1976) Evaluation Research in Education. New York: Irvington.

——— (1971) Multivariate Data Analysis. New York: John Wiley.

CRAMER, E. M. and W. A. NICEWANDER (1979) "Some symmetric, invariant measures of multivariate association." Psychometrika 44: 43-54.

CRONBACH, L. J. (1971) "Validity," in R. L. Thorndike (ed.) Educational Measurement. Washington, DC: American Council on Education.

————— (1957) "The two disciplines of scientific psychology." American Psychologist 12: 671-684.

DARLINGTON, R. B., S. L. WEINBERG, and H. J. WALBERG (1973) "Canonical variate analysis and related techniques." Review of Educational Research 43: 433-454.

DAWSON-SAUNDERS, B. K. (1982) "Correcting for bias in the canonical redundancy statistic." Educational and Psychological Measurement 42: 131-143

————— and D. R. DOOLEN (1981) "An alternative method to predict performance: Canonical redundancy analysis." Journal of Medical Education 56: 295-300.

DeSARBO, W. S. (1981) "Canonical/redundancy factoring analysis." Psychometrika 46: 307-329.

EDWARDS, A. L. (1979) Multiple Regression and the Analysis of Variance and Covariance. San Francisco: Freeman.

FORNELL, C. [ed.] (1982) A Second Generation of Multivariate Analysis (vol. 2). New York: Praeger.

————— (1978) "Three approaches to canonical analysis." Journal of the Market Research Society 20: 166-181.

GLASS, G. V, B. McGAW, and M. L. SMITH (1981) Meta-Analysis in Social Research. Beverly Hills, CA: Sage.

GORSUCH, R. L. (1974) Factor Analysis. Philadelphia: Saunders.

GREEN, P. E. (1978) Mathematical Tools for Applied Multivariate Analysis. New York: Academic Press.

GUILFORD, J. P. Fundamental Statistics in Psychology and Education. New York: McGraw-Hill.

GULLIKSEN, H. (1968) "Methods for determining equivalence of measures." Psychological Bulletin 70: 534-544.

HAYS, W. (1963) Statistics. New York: Holt, Rinehart & Winston.

HICKS, C. R. (1973) Fundamental Concepts in the Design of Experiments. New York: Holt, Rinehart & Winston.

HOMANS, G. C. (1967) The Nature of Social Science. New York: Harcourt, Brace & World.

HORST, P. (1961) "Generalized canonical correlations and their applications to experimental data." Journal of Clinical Psychology 26: 331-347.

HOTELLING, H. (1935) "The most predictable criterion." Journal of Experimental Psychology 26: 139-142.

HUBA, G. J., M. D. NEWCOMB, and P. M. BENTLER (1981) "Comparison of canonical correlation and interbattery factor analysis on sensation seeking and drug use domains." Applied Psychological Measurement 5: 291-306.

HUBA, G. J., A. L. PALISOC, and P. M. BENTLER (1982) "ORSIM2: A FORTRAN program for symmetric and asymmetric orthogonal rotation of canonical variates and interbattery factors." American Statistician 36: 62.

HUBA, G. J., J. A. WINGARD, and P. M. BENTLER (1980) "Longitudinal analysis of the role of peer support, adult models, and peer subcultures in beginning adolescent substance use: An application of setwise canonical correlation methods." Multivariate Behavioral Research 15: 259-280.

HUCK, S. W., W. H. CORMIER, and W. G. BOUNDS, Jr. (1974) Reading Statistics in Research. New York: Harper & Row.

JAIN, A. K. (1972) "CANCOR: Program for canonical correlation of three or more sets of variables." Journal of Marketing Research 9: 69-70.

66

JOHANSSON, J. K. (1981) "An extension of Wollenberg's redundancy analysis." Psychometrika 46: 93-103.

KAISER, H. F. (1970) "A second generation little jiffy." Psychometrika 35: 401-415.

———— (1956) "The varimax method of factor analysis." Doctoral dissertation, University of California, Berkeley.

————, S. HUNKA, and J. BIANCHINI (1969) "Relating factors between studies based upon different individuals," pp. 333-343 in H. J. Eysenck and S.B.G. Eysenck (eds.) Personality Structure and Measurement. San Diego: Knapp.

KERLINGER, F. N. (1973) Foundations of Behavioral Research. New York: Holt, Rinehart & Winston.

————and E. J. PEDHAZUR (1973) Multiple Regression in Behavioral Research. New York: Holt, Rinehart & Winston.

KIM, J. (1975) "Factor analysis." In N. H. Nie et al. (eds.) Statistical Package for the Social Sciences. New York: McGraw-Hill.

KNAPP, T. R. (1978) "Canonical correlation analysis: A general parametric significance-testing system." Psychological Bulletin 85: 410-416.

KRUS, D. J., T. S. REYNOLDS, and P. H. KRUS (1976) "Rotation in canonical variate analysis." Educational and Psychological Measurement 36: 725-730.

KUYLEN, A.A.A., and T.M.M. VERHALLEN (1981) "The use of canonical analysis." Journal of Economic Psychology 1: 217-237.

LEE, S. (1978) "Generalizations of the partial, part and bipartial canonical correlation analysis." Psychometrika 43: 427-431.

LEVINE, M. S. (1977) Canonical Analysis and Factor Comparison. Beverly Hills, CA: Sage.

LONG, J. M. (1974) "An extension of stepwise variable-reduction procedures for canonical analysis." Doctoral dissertation, University of Illinois at Urbana-Champaign. Dissertation Abstracts International, 1975, 35, 7128A. (University Microfilms No. 75-11,663)

McLAUGHLIN, S. D. and L. B. OTTO (1981) "Canonical correlation analysis in family research." Journal of Marriage and the Family 43: 7-16.

MARASCUILO, L. A. and J. R. LEVIN (1983) "Multivariate statistics in the social sciences: A researcher's guide." Monterey, CA: Brooks/Cole.

MAXWELL, A. E. (1961) "Canonical variate analysis when the variables are dichotomous." Educational and Psychological Measurement 21: 259-271.

MEREDITH, W. (1964) "Canonical correlations with fallible data." Psychometrika 29: 55-65.

MILLER, J. K. (1975) "The sampling distribution and a test for the significance of the bimultivariate redundancy statistic: A Monte Carlo study." Multivariate Behavioral Research 10: 233-244.

MORROW, J. R., Jr. and R. G. FRANKIEWICZ (1979) "Strategies for the analysis of repeated and multiple measures designs." Research Quarterly 50: 297-304.

MULLER, K. E. (1981) "Relationships between redundancy analysis, canonical correlation, and multivariate regression." Psychometrika 46: 139-142.

NUNNALLY, J. C. (1967) Psychometric Theory. New York: McGraw-Hill.

PING, C. and L. R. TUCKER (1976) "Transformation of both predictor and criterion variables to a simplified regression structure." Presented at the annual meeting of the American Educational Research Association, San Francisco. (ERIC Document Reproduction Service, ED 121 809)

PITTS, M. C. and B. THOMPSON (1984) "Cognitive styles as mediating variables in inferential comprehension." Reading Research Quarterly 19: 426-435.

RADER, B. T. (1975) "The application of canonical correlation methodology with vocational education data." Journal of Industrial Teacher Education 12: 51-61.

RAO, B. R. (1951) "An asymptotic expansion of the distribution of Wilks's criterion." Bulletin of the International Statistics Institute 33: 177-180.

REYNOLDS, T. J. and E. F. JACKOSFSKY (1981) "Interpreting canonical analysis: The use of orthogonal transformations." Educational and Psychological Measurement 41: 661-671.

RIM, E. (1972) "A stepwise canonical approach to the selection of 'kernel' variables from two sets of variables." Doctoral dissertation, University of Illinois at Urbana—Champaign, 1972. Dissertation Abstracts International, 1973, 34, 623A. (University Microfilms No. 73-17,386)

STAVIG, G. R. and A. C. ACOCK (1981) "Applying the semistandardized regression coefficient to factor, canonical, and path analysis." Multivariate Behavioral Research 16: 207-213.

STEWART, D. K. and W. A. LOVE (1968) "A general canonical correlation index." Psychological Bulletin 70: 160-163.

TATE, R. L. (1982) "Generalized canonical correlation analysis: An illustration." Presented at the annual meeting of the American Educational Research Association, New York.

TATSUOKA, M. M. (1973) "Multivariate analysis in educational research," in F. N. Kerlinger (ed.) Review of Research in Education. Itasca, IL: Peacock.

——— (1971) Multivariate Analysis: Techniques for Educational and Psychological Research. New York: John Wiley.

———(1969) Validation Studies: The Use of Multiple Regression Equations. Champaign, IL: Institute for Personality and Ability Testing.

THOMPSON, B. (1982a) "CANBAK: A computer program which performs stepwise canonical correlation analysis." Educational and Psychological Measurement 42: 849-851.

——— (1982b) "Comparison of two methods for computing canonical invariance coefficients." Presented at the annual meeting of the Southwest Educational Research Association, Austin. (Order document 03991, National Auxiliary Publication Service, P.O. Box 3513, Grand Central Station, New York, NY 10017)

——— (1982c) "Factor analysis based on 'doubly-centered' raw data matrices." Presented at the annual meeting of the Southwest Educational Research Association, Austin. (ERIC Document Reproduction Service, ED 219 404)

——— (1982d) "A logic for stepwise canonical correlation analysis." Perceptual and Motor Skills 54: 879-882.

———(1982e) "Stepwise canonical correlation analysis." Presented at the annual meeting of the Southwest Educational Research Association, Austin.

———(1981a) "The problem of OVAism." Presented at the annual meeting of the Mid-South Educational Research Association, Lexington. (Order document 03980, National Auxiliary Publication Service, P.O. Box 3513, Grand Central Station, New York, NY 10017)

———(1981b) "Utility of invariance coefficients." Perceptual and Motor Skills 52: 708-710.

68

———— (1980a) "Canonical correlation: Recent extensions for modelling educational processes." Presented at the annual meeting of the American Educational Research Association, Boston. (ERIC Document Reproduction Service, ED 199 269)

———— (1980b) "The instructional strategy decisions of teachers." Education 101: 150-157.

———— and G. M. BORRELLO (in press) "The importance of structure coefficients in regression research." Educational and Psychological Measurement.

THOMPSON, B. and R. G. FRANKIEWICZ (1979) "CANON: A computer program which produces canonical structure and index coefficients." Educational and Psychological Measurement 39: 219-222.

THOMPSON, B. and A. H. MILLER (1978) "Dissonance theory and education students' attitudes toward teachers." Journal of Experimental Education 47: 55-59.

THOMPSON, B. and R. RUCKER (1980) "Two-year college students' goals and program preferences." Journal of College Student Personnel 21: 393-398.

THORNDIKE, R. M. (1978) Correlational Procedures for Research. New York: Gardner.

———— (1977) "Canonical analysis and predictor selection." Journal of Multivariate Behavioral Research 12: 75-87.

———— (1976a) "Strategies for rotating canonical components." Presented at the annual meeting of the American Educational Research Association, San Francisco. (ERIC Document Reproduction Service, ED 123 259)

———— (1976b) "Studying canonical analysis: Comments on Barcikowski and Stevens." Multivariate Behavioral Research 11: 249-253.

———— and D. J. WEISS (1973) "A study of the stability of canonical correlations and canonical components." Educational and Psychological Measurement 33: 123-184.

THURSTONE, L. L. (1947) Multiple Factor Analysis. Chicago: University of Chicago Press.

———— (1935) The Vectors of the Mind. Chicago: University of Chicago Press.

TIMM, N. H. (1975) Multivariate Analysis with Applications in Education and Psychology. Monterey, CA: Brooks/Cole.

————and J. E. CARLSON (1976) "Part and bipartial canonical correlation analysis." Psychometrika 41: 159-176.

VELDMAN, D. J. (1967) FORTRAN Programming for the Behavioral Sciences. New York: Holt, Rinehart & Winston.

WEINBERG, S. L. and R. B. DARLINGTON (1976) "Canonical analysis when number of variables is large relative to sample size." Journal of Educational Statistics 1: 313-332.

WILKINSON, L. (1977) "Confirmatory rotation of MANOVA canonical variates." Multivariate Behavioral Research 12: 487-494.

WILLSON, V. L. (1982) "Misuses of regression approaches to ANOVA and ANCOVA." Presented at the annual meeting of the Southwest Educational Research Association, Austin.

———— (1980) "Research techniques in AERJ articles: 1969 to 1975." Educational Researcher 9: 5-10.

WIMMER, R. (1977) "Canonical correlation/factor analysis; Similarities and differences." Journal of Organizational Behavior 21: 211-213.

WOLLENBERG, A. L. VAN DEN (1977) "Redundancy analysis: An alternative for canonical correlation analysis." Psychometrika 42: 207-219.

WOOD, D. A. and J. A. ERSKINE (1976) "Strategies in canonical correlation with application to behavioral data." Educational and Psychological Measurement 36: 861-878.

ZINKGRAF, S. A. (1983) "Performing factorial multivariate analysis of variance using canonical correlation analysis." Educational and Psychological Measurement 43: 63-68.

BRUCE THOMPSON is Associate Dean and Associate Professor of Education at the University of New Orleans. He previously served as an Assistant Director of the Research and Program Evaluation Department in the Houston Independent School District. He completed his doctoral training at the University of Houston in 1978 and is the author of some four dozen articles.

$5.00 each

Quantitative Applications in the Social Sciences

A SAGE UNIVERSITY PAPER SERIES

SPECIAL OFFER
(on prepaid orders only)

Order all 56
for $210.00
and save $70.00

*brief, clearly
articulated
explanations of
advanced
methodological
concepts good
for classroom,
professional
and library use . . .*

SAGE PUBLICATIONS
Beverly Hills
London
New Delhi

ORDER CARD

Quantitative Applications in the Social Sciences

A SAGE UNIVERSITY PAPER SERIES

Name _____

Address _____

City _____ State _____ Zip _____

☐ I want to take advantage of your **Prepaid Special Offer.**
   ☐ Please send me all 56 papers at the *prepaid* price of $210.00.

My check or money order is enclosed.

This Special Offer available in the U.S. and Canada only.

☐ Please send me the Sage Papers checked below at the regular price of $5.00 each.

- ☐ 1. **Analysis of Variance** *Iversen/Norpoth*
- ☐ 2. **Operations Research Methods** *Nagel/Neef*
- ☐ 3. **Causal Modeling, 2nd Edition** *Asher*
- ☐ 4. **Tests of Significance** *Henkel*
- ☐ 5. **Cohort Analysis** *Glenn*
- ☐ 6. **Canonical Analysis & Factor Comparison** *Levine*
- ☐ 7. **Analysis of Nominal Data, 2nd Edition** *Reynolds*
- ☐ 8. **Analysis of Ordinal Data** *Hildebrand/Laing/Rosenthal*
- ☐ 9. **Time Series Analysis: Regression Techniques** *Ostrom*
- ☐ 10. **Ecological Inference** *Langbein/Lichtman*
- ☐ 11. **Multidimensional Scaling** *Kruskal/Wish*
- ☐ 12. **Analysis of Covariance** *Wildt/Ahtola*
- ☐ 13. **Introduction to Factor Analysis** *Kim/Mueller*
- ☐ 14. **Factor Analysis** *Kim/Mueller*
- ☐ 15. **Multiple Indicators: An Introduction** *Sullivan/Feldman*
- ☐ 16. **Exploratory Data Analysis** *Hartwig/Dearing*
- ☐ 17. **Reliability & Validity Assessment** *Carmines/Zeller*
- ☐ 18. **Analyzing Panel Data** *Markus*
- ☐ 19. **Discriminant Analysis** *Klecka*
- ☐ 20. **Log-Linear Models** *Knoke/Burke*
- ☐ 21. **Interrupted Time Series Analysis** *McDowall/McCleary/Meidinger/Hay*
- ☐ 22. **Applied Regression: An Introduction** *Lewis-Beck*
- ☐ 23. **Research Designs** *Spector*
- ☐ 24. **Unidimensional Scaling** *McIver/Carmines*
- ☐ 25. **Magnitude Scaling: Quantitative Measurement of Opinions** *Lodge*
- ☐ 26. **Multiattribute Evaluation** *Edwards/Newman*
- ☐ 27. **Dynamic Modeling** *Huckfeldt/Kohfeld/Likens*
- ☐ 28. **Network Analysis** *Knoke/Kuklinski*
- ☐ 29. **Interpreting and Using Regression** *Achen*
- ☐ 30. **Test Item Bias** *Osterlind*
- ☐ 31. **Mobility Tables** *Hout*
- ☐ 32. **Measures of Association** *Liebetrau*
- ☐ 33. **Confirmatory Factor Analysis: A Preface to LISREL** *Long*
- ☐ 34. **Covariance Structure Models: An Introduction to LISREL** *Long*
- ☐ 35. **Introduction to Survey Sampling** *Kalton*
- ☐ 36. **Achievement Testing: Recent Advances** *Bejar*
- ☐ 37. **Nonrecursive Causal Models** *Berry*
- ☐ 38. **Matrix Algebra: An Introduction** *Namboodiri*
- ☐ 39. **Introduction to Applied Demography** *Rives/Serow*
- ☐ 40. **Microcomputer Methods for Social Scientists** *Schrodt*
- ☐ 41. **Game Theory: Concepts and Applications** *Zagare*
- ☐ 42. **Using Published Data: Errors and Remedies** *Jacob*
- ☐ 43. **Bayesian Statistical Inference** *Iversen*
- ☐ 44. **Cluster Analysis** *Aldenderfer/Blashfield*
- ☐ 45. **Linear Probability, Logit, and Probit Models** *Aldrich/Nelson*
- ☐ 46. **Event History Analysis: Regression for Longitudinal Event Data** *Allison*
- ☐ 47. **Canonical Correlation Analysis: Uses and Interpretation** *Thompson*
- ☐ 48. **Models for Innovation Diffusion** *Mahajan/Peterson*
- ☐ 49. **Basic Content Analysis** *Weber*
- ☐ 50. **Multiple Regression in Practice** *Berry/Feldman*
- ☐ 51. **Stochastic Parameter Regression Models** *Newbold/Bos*
- ☐ 52. **Using Microcomputers in Research** *Madron/Tate/Brookshire*
- ☐ 53. **Secondary Analysis of Survey Data** *Kiecolt/Nathan*
- ☐ 54. **Multivariate Analysis of Variance** *Bray/Maxwell*
- ☐ 55. **The Logic of Causal Order** *Davis*
- ☐ 56. **Introduction to Linear Goal Programming** *Ignizio*

*Orders under $20 MUST be prepaid. California residents add 6% sales tax.
All prices subject to change without notice.*

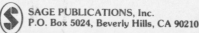

SAGE PUBLICATIONS, Inc.
P.O. Box 5024, Beverly Hills, CA 90210

Quantitative Applications
in the Social Sciences

(a Sage University Papers Series)

$5.00 each

SAGE PUBLICATIONS, INC.
P.O. BOX 5024
BEVERLY HILLS, CALIFORNIA 90210

Place
Stamp
here